A NATURAL LANGUAGE INTERFACE FOR COMPUTER-AIDED DESIGN

THE KLUWER INTERNATIONAL SERIES IN ENGINEERING AND COMPUTER SCIENCE

NATURAL LANGUAGE PROCESSING AND MACHINE TRANSLATION

Consulting Editor

Jaime Carbonell

A NATURAL LANGUAGE INTERFACE FOR COMPUTER-AIDED DESIGN

by

Tariq Samad
Carnegie-Mellon University
Research Center for Computer Aided Design

KLUWER ACADEMIC PUBLISHERS
Boston / Dordrecht / Lancaster

Distributors for North America:
Kluwer Academic Publishers
101 Philip Drive
Assinippi Park
Norwell, Massachusetts 02061, USA

Distributors for the UK and Ireland:
Kluwer Academic Publishers
MTP Press Limited
Falcon House, Queen Square
Lancaster LA1 1RN, UNITED KINGDOM

Distributors for all other countries:
Kluwer Academic Publishers Group
Distribution Centre
Post Office Box 322
3300 AH Dordrecht, THE NETHERLANDS

Library of Congress Cataloging-in-Publication Data

Samad, Tariq.
A natural language interface for computer aided design.

(Kluwer international series in engineering and computer science)
Includes index.
1. Engineering design—Data processing.
2. Computer-aided design. 3. CLEOPATRA (Computer program language) I. Title. II. Series.
TA174.S24 1986 620′.00425′02855133 86-9407
ISBN 0-89838-222-X

Printed in the United States of America

Contents

Preface

The advent of computer aided design and the proliferation of computer aided design tools have been instrumental in furthering the state-of-the-art in integrated circuitry. Continuing this progress, however, demands an emphasis on creating user-friendly environments that facilitate the interaction between the designer and the CAD tool. The realization of this fact has prompted investigations into the appropriateness for CAD of a number of user-interface technologies. One type of interface that has hitherto not been considered is the natural language interface. It is our contention that natural language interfaces could solve many of the problems posed by the increasing number and sophistication of CAD tools.

This thesis represents the first step in a research effort directed towards the eventual development of a natural language interface for the domain of computer aided design. The breadth and complexity of the CAD domain renders the task of developing a natural language interface for the complete domain beyond the scope of a single doctoral thesis. Hence, we have initally focussed on a sub-domain of CAD. Specifically, we have developed a natural language interface, named Cleopatra, for circuit-simulation post-processing. In other words, with Cleopatra a circuit-designer can extract and manipulate, in English, values from the output of a circuit-simulator (currently *SPICE*) without manually having to go through the output files produced by the simulator.

A second consequence of the breadth and complexity of the CAD domain is that extensibility is of paramount concern. For Cleopatra to be a successful foundation for an ambitious research program, we cannot afford to impose a priori restrictions on Cleopatra's underlying formalism. In contrast, much prior work on natural language interfaces has been directed towards narrow or "toy" domains. Since extensibility to larger domains has seldom been a consideration in previous interfaces, the seriousness of their limitations has appeared mitigated.

Cleopatra, therefore, is based on an approach to natural language understanding that we have developed that is distinct from previous approaches. This approach extends what is in essence a case-frame parser with a couple of novel features: high degrees of flexibility and parallelism, the latter supplemented with a notion of "confidence-levels". These features have enabled us to handle constructions that are generally beyond the scope of "pure" case-frame parsers without forsaking the intuitive appeal of case-frame semantics.

Presentations and demonstrations of Cleopatra have been received with much enthusiasm, and we are confident that when "field tested" in the near future, Cleopatra will prove to be a useful CAD tool in its own right, and that it will demonstrate that even for sophisticated domains such as computer aided design, the natural language interface is a technology whose time has come.

There are many people whose encouragement and advice have contributed to this research:

First and foremost, I would like to thank my thesis advisor, Professor Stephen W. Director, for his continual support and encouragement during my years at C-MU, and for his willingness to indulge me in what began as an interdisciplinary pursuit of uncertain merit.

I would like to thank Professors Jaime Carbonell, David Evans, and Dan Siewiorek for serving on my thesis committee and for their helpful suggestions. Dan Siewiorek suggested that I discuss the domain of behavioral-simulation post-processing as a possible extension of this work; David Evans has been instrumental in making my linguistic naivety less evident in the dissertation; and both he and Jaime Carbonell have been extremely supportive of my work since its inception.

This final document has benefitted greatly from comments by Steve Director on many earlier drafts, and also from careful readings by David Evans, Tom Cobourn, and Karen Nemchik. I would also like to acknowledge Tom's discoveries of numerous deficiencies (many were more than just "bugs") in Cleopatra.

Michael Bushnell has been a valuable source of advice on subjects ranging from status codes in Franz LISP to the semantic consequence of adverb position in English.

This research was supported in part by the Semiconductor Research Corporation under Contract Number 82-11-007.

Tariq Samad
Pittsburgh, Pennsylvania

A NATURAL LANGUAGE INTERFACE FOR COMPUTER-AIDED DESIGN

In the state of mind in which we "observe", we are a long way below the level to which we rise when we create.

Marcel Proust, *Remembrance of Things Past*

I said that the world is absurd, but I was too hasty. This world in itself is not reasonable, that is all that can be said. But what is absurd is the confrontation of this irrational and the wild longing for clarity whose call echoes in the human heart.

Albert Camus, *The Myth of Sisyphus*

Chapter 1
Introduction

State-of-the-art VLSI design has long since outstripped the abilities of the unaided designer, and we are now at a point where improvements in integrated circuits owe increasingly greater debts to the ensemble of computer-aided design tools. The "computer-aided designer" of today can utilize CAD tools at every stage of the design process, from behavioral and functional specification to process simulation and layout.

The potentials for higher productivity and for technological breakthroughs offered by the proliferation of CAD tools can hardly be overemphasized. However, shortfalls in the realizations of these potentials have led to the recognition that the need for making CAD tools easier to use is imperative. The lack of "user-friendliness" of CAD tools can be attributed to a number of factors, of which we would like to mention two in particular:

- Learning how to use a tool requires careful and detailed study of one or more manuals.This task is scarcely made easier by the (poor) expository quality exhibited in most manuals, or by the typical designer's eagerness (or lack thereof) to master arcane details.

- The outputs produced by CAD tools are often overwhelming. Circuit-simulators, for example, can produce hundreds of pages of output, and the small fraction of this information that is relevant to the designer may be scattered through the hundreds of pages.

Because such barriers to productive use of CAD tools have been recognized, there is growing interest in improved user-interfaces for CAD. Initially, user-interfaces were tool-specific, and prone to many of the shortcomings of the tools themselves as far as convenience of use and ease of learning is concerned. Recently, however, the post-facto design of particular interfaces for particular tools has given way to user-interfaces for CAD becoming a subject of research in their own right. A product of this research that has already proven beneficial is the menu-based interface (e.g. Delilah [8, 41]).

Menu-based interfaces provide considerable facility in dealing with CAD tools that can be characterized as having an argument structure for commands that is essentially linear. For graphics packages, for example, a menu-based interface is probably the most appropriate. However, for such CAD activities as extracting useful information from the output of a circuit-simulator, or accessing a data-base, a menu-based interface lacks the requisite expressive power. In the context of a design library, an intention such as *I want to find out if there are any full-adders in the CMOS library that have a maximum clock frequency greater than 50 MHz,* does not allow straightforward expression via menu-frames.

As the sophistication of CAD tools increases, and as the incorporation of artificial intelligence methods leads to integrated tools that address the higher-level design stages [21], the role of the IC designer will increasingly become that of an intelligent advisor communicating with an "intelligent" design environment. In such a situation, there may be no alternative to verbal interaction between the designer and the computer. Though, admittedly, a design environment of such power is not going to be available in the immediate future, it is not an overly fanciful conception; some recent research projects have just this object [19, 9, 55].

1.1. The Pros and Cons of Natural Language Interfaces

A part of the solution to the problems posed by present user-interfaces is, we feel, the development of a natural language interface, and it is to this end that the work described here has been directed. Computer-aided design could profit from a natural language interface in a number of ways:

- A natural language interface is not tool specific—the same natural language interface could be used with a variety of tools. A natural language interface can, therefore, obviate the need for the designer to memorize the particular formats of each tool. For a field that is as tool-intensive as CAD, this is an especially telling advantage that natural language holds over conventional modes of interaction.

- Use of a natural language interface does not require extensive perusal of a manual, or a major learning effort. (In fact, the ideal natural language interface would not require any learning effort.) Furthermore, the little effort that may be required is a one-time investment; it need not be repeated for each subsequent tool.

- A natural language interface provides a facility for "natural" expression. Unlike formal query languages, for example, a natural language interface does not require a verbal thought to be mentally translated into an unnatural formal language. Additionally, designers of natural language interfaces have a point in common with the intended users of the interfaces—they all speak the same language. A natural language interface is much more likely to contain the kinds of constructs users would consider desirable than conventional interfaces.

- Menu-based and keyword-based interfaces have severe limitations when it comes to some kinds of complex expressions. Natural language interfaces are less prone to such limitations. We saw one example of this earlier. To give another: It is difficult to imagine a conventional interface in which one could express what in English we can express readily as *Is there an output node with a voltage greater than 3 volts when the input goes high?*

While few would argue that natural language interfaces have advantages such as these, there seems to be a common perception that such advantages are outweighed by severe handicaps [65, 28, 57, 39]. In particular, such "features" of language as ambiguity and verbosity are considered to render natural language interfaces unacceptable for analytic tasks. We will later see that other features of language such as ellipsis and anaphora allow succinct expression, and that it is possible to utilize the linguistic context for disambiguation.

Criticisms of natural language for user-machine communication have generally not been based on empirical grounds. In fact, realized (as opposed to hypothetical or simulated) natural language interfaces have rarely been evaluated experimentally. To the best of our knowledge, only two experiments that compare performance between a realized natural language interface and a conventional interface have been reported [4, 47]. In both these experiments, the natural language interface received the better evaluation, on both subjective (user-preference) and objective (success-rate, efficiency) criteria.

1.2. Domanial Implications

Interest in natural language interfaces goes back at least twenty-odd years [33], and many approaches have been tried since. The study of previous natural language interfaces is a rich source of ideas, but it also underlines the deficiencies of previous approaches to natural language understanding, deficiencies that would be fatal in a complex real-world domain. The task of building a natural language interface for CAD, therefore, cannot be simply one of applying an existing technology to a new domain.

In contrast to previous natural language interfaces, most of which dealt with "toy" domains or, by self-admission, were never intended for "real" use, we cannot afford to delimit a subset of English as sufficient; the CAD domain is too large and too complex. An "intelligent" VLSI design environment could have as components many design data-bases, and synthesis and analysis tools at several levels of the design hierarchy. The components would be diverse, and each could make different demands of an interface. For a data-base, a question-answering facility is essential, and a manual-update facility might be useful, too; an analysis tool (such as a circuit-simulator) might need to perform actions (such as drawing graphs) on command; a synthesis tool might need to ask the user for advice if its knowledge is incomplete, and it might need to have an explanation facility.

For all these activities to reap full benefit from a natural language interface, it is essential that we refrain from letting convenience of implementation dictate the linguistic coverage of the interface. Again in contrast to previous natural language interfaces, the design of a natural language interface for CAD cannot be based on prior assumptions about which English constructions will be useful, and which will be useless; the diversity of the domain implies that all such assumptions stand in great danger of invalidation as the scope of the interface broadens over time.

In summary, the complexity and the diversity of the CAD domain, as well as the consequential importance of extensibility for a natural language interface for this domain, render previous approaches to natural language interfaces of little practical utility for our purposes. We need an approach of greater generality and power.

1.3. Cleopatra

The ultimate goal of our research is the development of a natural language interface for CAD, and this thesis describes a research effort that takes the first step towards that goal. We have constructed a natural language interface, christened Cleopatra[1], for the circuit-simulation post-processing sub-domain. Using Cleopatra, an IC designer can extract and manipulate, in English, the relevant values from the ouput of a circuit-simulator without physically poring through the output listing itself, and without the perusing of manuals that use of a more conventional interface would necessitate.

For readers unfamiliar with CAD, a circuit-simulator is a computer program that models the behavior of electronic circuits. The relevant inputs to a circuit-simulator are: a description of a circuit, the time-interval over which the simulation is to be performed, and the output variables (usually the voltages at particular nodes) the values of which are requested. The output produced by the circuit-simulator is a listing

---

[1] *a Comfortable Linguistic Environment that Ostensibly Permits Arbitrary Textual Requests and Assertions*, as forced an acronym as the best of them!

of, usually, the voltages at the nodes of interest at discrete time-points over the range of the specified time-interval. In the context of circuit-simulation post-processing, expressions such as *node* and *voltage* refer only to labels and numbers in the output listing, and not to concepts these expressions might denote in broader contexts.

Cleopatra reads a file that must be in the output format of a particular circuit-simulator (currently *SPICE* [54]). A circuit-simulator output-file can be considered a degenerate data-base; extracting useful information from such a file, just as much as from a full-fledged data-base, requires framing a "query." We have therefore limited Cleopatra's coverage to questions for the present. Assertions or commands, which are important in other CAD sub-domains, and which we have spent effort to ensure Cleopatra could be extended to handle, are of little importance in circuit-simulation post-processing.

The following queries, all of which Cleopatra can currently answer, illustrate what we mean by circuit-simulation post-processing:

After the voltage at n1 reaches 3 volts when is the voltage at n2 maximum?[2]

S1. When is the voltage at n1 greater than 3 volts when the voltage at n2 equals 5 volts?

S2. At 5 ns which node is the voltage the maximum at?

What are the voltages at n1 and n2 between 5 and 20 ns?

(In our illustrations of Cleopatra's input, we will show queries with

[2] *N1*, *n2*, etc. are node-identifiers.

conventional capitalization and punctuation. However, all input to Cleopatra has to be in the form of a list, and capitalization is disregarded [see Appendix A].)

Cleopatra incorporates an approach to natural language processing that is, we feel, much better suited for the CAD domain. Not only can we handle constructions that are often beyond the capabilities of natural language interfaces (for example, ***headless relative clauses*** [Sentence *(S1)*] and ***wh-frontings*** [Sentence *(S2)*]), but we are confident that other constructions can be added with facility as the need arises.

Cleopatra consists of about 7000 lines of Franz Lisp [29] code, and runs on a VAX 11/785 under 4.2 BSD UNIX.

1.4. Natural Language Processing—Some Preliminaries

We describe here the components of a conventional natural language processing system, and our reasons for attending mainly to the parsing component.

The computational "understanding" of natural language can be thought of as a sequence of operations. The first operation corresponds to a *parser*, which is a procedure that takes as input a natural language sentence (more generally, a natural language fragment), and outputs an explicit, unambiguous, structured representation (the *parsed representation*) of the sentence. Parsers usually utilize mainly syntactic information (the *grammar*). If the parsed representation does not reflect the meaning relationships of the constituents of the sentence, a *semantic component* may be required that converts the parsed representation into a *semantic structure*. Finally, the *pragmatics component* is responsible for such tasks as identifying the referents of referring expressions (anaphora) and for recognizing the intentions behind the production of the sentence. (Such intentions can include updating a knowledge-base, requesting information, running a program, etc.)

A short example should help to distinguish between syntax, semantics, and pragmatics. Consider the sentence:

Simulate the ALU with SPICE.

At the syntactic level this sentence is analyzed (partially) as follows: *Simulate* is a verb, *the ALU* is a definite noun phrase, *with SPICE* is a prepositional phrase. With semantic information this can be refined to: *the ALU* is the object of the simulation, *SPICE* is the instrument of the simulation. Finally, the pragmatics component is used to determine which ALU *the ALU* refers to, and for recognizing the sentence as a command to invoke SPICE to simulate the ALU. (The pragmatics component might well initiate the simulation.)

This thesis is concerned mainly with the parsing component, though we devote a later chapter to a discussion of Cleopatra's semantic component, and towards the end we briefly mention some pragmatics issues. Our concern with parsing, at the expense of semantics and pragmatics, can be justified on three counts:

- The parsing process conceptually precedes both the semantics and the pragmatics processes. This does not imply that the parsing process must be run to completion before any semantic information is brought to bear—there are good arguments against that, as we shall see. In fact, semantic and pragmatic information can be applied during the parsing process, for instance in judgements of meaningfulness; but the semantics component and the pragmatics component will only "see" structures that have gone through the parser.

- Cleopatra's parsing process employs a high degree of generality and power. In fact, we can incorporate into the parsing process information that in most natural language interfaces is localized to the semantics or pragmatics phase. We will see examples of the utilization of semantic information throughout the discussion of the parser, and later we will mention a pragmatics issue that can be handled within Cleopatra's parser.

- Narrowness of domain seems to simplify the later phases of the understanding process more than the parsing phase. Our domain of interest is the narrow, circumscripted one of circuit-simulation post-processing. We are not claiming that the pragmatics and the semantics components are rendered trivial in this domain, but that the pragmatics and the semantics required for as limited a sub-domain as ours are very small subsets of the pragmatics and semantics required generally. The subsetting afforded the parsing process by the narrowness of domain, on the other hand, is not nearly so drastic. This consideration allows us some optimism that Cleopatra's parser will be upgradable as the domain-limitations are relaxed, whereas the pragmatics component, if one had been implemented, would have been obsolescent from its inception.

1.5. An Outline of this Thesis

Many different approaches to natural language understanding have been attempted, as we said earlier. We will review some of these approaches in the next chapter, pointing out their advantages and disadvantages. Our work differs from previous approaches in its espousal of two features, flexibility and parallelism, which together yield the generality and power of Cleopatra. We discuss these features in Chapter 3, demonstrating their importance and their implementation in our work.

A consequence of our emphasis on generality and power is that a detailed step-by-step description of the parsing process employed by Cleopatra would be prohibitively complicated. We discuss the architecture of Cleopatra in Chapter 4, but in order to keep digressions to a minimum we will leave some gaps in this discussion. Most of these gaps are filled in the following chapter, in which we also discuss Cleopatra's handling of conjunctions and ellipses. Chapter 6 concludes the discussion of Cleopatra's parsing process by exhaustively analyzing the parsing of three representative sentences.

After a natural language input has been parsed, a response has to be calculated. This operation is performed by the semantic interpretation process, and is discussed in Chapter 7.

We discuss some issues for future work in Chapter 8, and we conclude this thesis with a brief discussion of some relevant philosophical issues. Two appendices are also included: the transcript of a sample terminal session, and an exercise in the extension of Cleopatra's linguistic coverage.

Chapter 2
Previous Approaches

In this chapter we discuss some approaches to natural language processing that researchers have taken. Our intention here is not to conduct a detailed examination of all previous work in natural language processing, but rather to introduce some issues and features of importance for natural language interfaces, and to discuss some relevant approaches *vis a vis* these issues.

One important issue is how syntactic and semantic processing should be coordinated in the parsing process. Most approaches can be characterized by the relative significance they assign to syntax versus semantics. On the one extreme we find approaches where all the syntactic processing is completed before any semantic information is brought to bear. This reflects the practice in much linguistic theory to treat syntax autonomously [14, 70, 31]. For practical natural language interfaces, however, early consideration of semantics is a must, and there has been little work in developing natural language interfaces with a purely syntactic parsing component. Nevertheless we discuss the advantages and disadvantages of syntax-first approaches; this will prepare the ground, so to speak, for discussing more realistic approaches, and it will give us a point of reference that will be helpful for comparative purposes.

At the other extreme are approaches that use semantic information extensively (and sometimes exclusively) throughout the parsing process. As can be expected perhaps, some of the pros and cons of each of these extremes complement each other. Natural language interfaces that emphasize semantic information usually do so at the expense of irregular coverage of syntactic constructions.

All the other approaches have a pragmatic cast to them, and they often borrow features from one extreme or the other. For example, to anticipate some nomenclature that will be defined later, augmented transition networks usually make use of syntactic grammars, whereas some case-frame parsers integrate features of Conceptual Dependency (an approach that relies primarily on semantic information) with a pattern-matcher.

2.1. Syntax-First approaches

Some theories of natural language understanding rely on an initial phase of purely syntactic processing, the output of which is then fed to a semantic interpreter, which yields the required representation. The syntactic processing is done according to a (syntactic) grammar—a grammar that deals with traditional parts-of-speech categories: nouns, noun-phrases, prepositions, etc. Some "subcategorization" may be done, but this will also be on a syntactic basis, e.g. dividing verbs into intransitives, transitives, and ditransitives; dividing nouns into count, abstract, and mass nouns, etc. Much work in parsing theory, especially work following the Chomskyan tradition, has focussed primarily on syntax devoid of semantic considerations.

There are definite advantages in leaving semantic considerations until a later phase of the understanding process. Languages exhibit a variety of syntactic constructions, and sometimes the choice of construction has little to do with meaning (though "stylistics" may often be a factor). For example, most active sentences are synonymous with the corresponding passives; *there*-insertion does not seem to change meaning (*A man is in the room* vs. *There is a man in the room*); and the dative construction can be used interchangeably with the direct object, indirect object construction (*John gave the dog to Mary* vs. *John gave Mary the dog*).

By separating syntax from semantics, the linguist (or the natural language interface developer) is free to incorporate all the syntactic constructions he cares to. Furthermore, since the traditional parts of speech are few and form an inextensible set, adding new words does not require adding new rules, but just additions to the dictionary.

The disadvantages of syntax-first approaches are definite, too. What may seem to be semantics-preserving syntactic constructions are sometimes, on closer deliberation, seen to be semantically motivated. Kiparsky and Kiparsky's semantic explication of complement sentences [45] is a good example.

Another problem with syntax-first approaches is their handling of ambiguity. Ambiguity thoroughly pervades language (see [72], where twenty classes of structural ambiguity are enumerated), and early application of semantic constraints is essential in order to reject spurious parses promptly. Because of the pervasion of ambiguity, a parser without access to semantic information is grossly underconstrained, and a semantics component that is invoked after a semantics-free parsing procedure is grossly overworked. Consider the sentence:

> John saw the convertible with California plates walking down the street.

Syntactically, this sentence is at least ten ways ambiguous, and a syntactic parser would produce ten parses that a semantic component would have to consider. On the other hand, if semantic information could be brought to bear as the parse progressed, only one interpretation would be ultimately produced, and some of the syntactically possible interpretations would not even be considered. The semantic information required here is that neither a convertible nor a plate can walk; that a plate cannot be an instrument of seeing (as, for example, a telescope can), and that convertibles do not have dinnerware. By embellishing syntactic grammars with *semantic features* in one form or another, some of the problems of ambiguity can be rendered tractable. For example, *John* can have the feature *animate*, and the verb *see* can require that its subject have the feature *animate*. (Semantic features are generally at the level of *human*, *animate*, etc.) In the next chapter, we will discuss a couple of shortcomings of semantic-features.

Grammars, by definition, enforce grammaticality. Syntactic grammars will not produce any output if some rule is violated. People, however, often use semantic clues to understand syntactically deviant sentences:

*I wanted that John win the game.[3]

*I hurt me.

*John to Bill the book gave.

[3]We follow the convention, standard in linguistic literature, of prefixing ungrammatical sentences by asterisks.

2.2. Semantic Grammars

At present, semantic grammars are probably the most popular technique for constructing natural language interfaces. A semantic grammar [7] is a set of context-free rewrite rules in which the non-terminal categories are domain-dependent semantic ones, and not the traditional syntactic ones (such as noun phrase, verb phrase, etc.).[4]

An example of a semantic grammar rule is:

S3. INFO-REQ —> what
<be-form> <measurement> <parameter>

This rule can be interpreted as: An information-request consists of the word *what*, a form of the verb *be*, a *measurement* phrase, and a *parameter* phrase, in that order. Queries such as the following could be accepted by this rule:

S4. What is the voltage at n2?

S5. What is the power-dissipation in Q1[5]?

A number of reasonably successful systems have been developed using semantic grammars [7, 73, 10]. In limited domains, and when extensibility to broader domains is not a factor, semantic grammars can elegantly capture the "meaning" of a sentence in a single phase.

---

[4]It is worth pointing out that a semantic grammar is *not* just any kind of grammar that utilizes semantic information in some arbitrary fashion.

[5]*Q1* refers to a transistor.

So-called "substitutional ellipsis" can be handled elegantly as well. The following example is from the XCALIBUR system [10]:

> What is the price of the three largest single-port fixed disks?
>
> Speed?

By recognizing that *price* is the only term of the same category as *speed* in the first question, a natural language understanding system can easily answer the second query by substituting *speed* for *price* in the first.

As mentioned before, semantic grammars are only good for restricted domains. A semantic grammar for any domain of reasonable complexity would require so many non-terminal categories (such as *<measurement>* and *<parameter>* in *(S3)*) and, therefore, so many rules, that its implementation would be unfeasible.

The structure of semantic grammars is restricted to context-free rules. Rule *(S3)* would not only parse sentences *(S4)* and *(S5)*, it would also accept nonsense such as the sentence:

> What is the power-dissipation at n2?

(Transistors can dissipate power, but nodes cannot.)

Syntactic grammars would also allow such utterances, but in a syntax-first approach a hypothetical semantic component would rule this out; in a semantic grammar, rules such as *(S3)* constitute the semantic component and, therefore, bear the full burden of pruning ungrammaticality.

On the other hand, a sentence superficially similar to *(S4)* or *(S5)* would require a separate rule (since a *file* is not a *measurement*):

S6. What is the longest file in my directory?

Furthermore, semantic grammars are never "transformational." That is, there is no way to relate synonymous sentences through rules. Active/passive and dative/ditransitive pairs would have to be handled through (separate) pairs of rules, and the close semantic relationship between the individual elements of such pairs would not be reflected in the grammar. The recognition of synonymous sentences can be effected only through multiple rules. Even worse, the same set of multiple rules as those for sentences synonymous with *(S4)* and *(S5)*, would have to be replicated, with minor changes, to allow analogously synonymous sentences for *(S6)*.

2.3. Augmented Transition Networks

Another formalism that enjoys a high degree of popularity among researchers in natural language processing is the augmented transition network, or ATN [80]. ATN's are finite-state transition diagrams with a couple of added features: Recursion is allowed, and arbitrary tests and actions on the arcs are allowed. (These additions make ATN's Turing-equivalent [3;p.266].) An ATN is a parsing architecture more than a grammar formalism. Thus, ATN's have been used in natural language interfaces based on non-domain-specific grammars [81, 6] as well as in interfaces based on semantic grammars [7, 73, 38].

ATN's based on syntactic grammars are not prey to the limitation of a narrow domain to the extent that all semantic-grammar-based systems are. In fact, interfaces with the broadest coverage have used ATN's

[81, 6]. On the other hand, constructions that cannot be conveniently expressed as rules of the grammar are difficult to handle. Phenomema such as ungrammaticality, ellipsis, and conjunctions all require taking a broader view of a parsing situation than a state in an ATN can provide. In fact, there is information encoded in the sequence of ATN states that have been instantiated, and this information is not available in the particular state in which some deviation from the grammar is recognized (see [11]). This does not mean that handling such phenomena are impossible within the ATN framework—in fact, some limited success has been achieved towards this end [46, 76]; however, ATN's suffer from not providing some kind of a meta-rule capability, and some such capability has to be tacked on in order to provide ATN-based systems the necessary power.

2.4. Case-Frame Parsing

Case-frame parsing borrows from the notions of case grammar (as elaborated by Fillmore [26]), and frame-based representation [53]. In case-grammar, a sentence is viewed as consisting of a verb, and nominal constituents, called *cases*, associated with the verb. Each verb has a set of *case-roles*, such as *subject*, *object*, *instrument*, and *locative*, which are identified with particular cases in the sentence. Frames are data-structures which have *slots* in which information about aspects of the frame can be stored. In case-frame parsing, verbs are represented as *verb-frames*, which have *case-role-slots* which *case-frames* (which represent cases) can *fill* [12].

For example, consider the sentences:

S7. John broke the window with a hammer.

S8. A hammer broke the window.

S9. John broke the window.

In these sentences, the case-frame corresponding to *the hammer* (where present) fills the slot for the *instrument* case-role for the verb-frame corresponding to the verb *break*, the case-frame for *the window* fills the *object* slot, and the case-frame for *John* (where present) fills the *agent* or *subject* slot. By utilizing constraints on the slot-fillers (for example, that the agent for *break* must be animate, and that the instrument for *break* must be an inanimate, portable, physical object), the cases can be correctly assigned when syntactic information is ambiguous. (For example, in *(S7)* and *(S9)*, *John* is the syntactic subject and fills the *subject* or *agent* case-roles; in *(S8) the hammer* is the syntactic subject and fills the *instrument* case-role.)

Case-frame parsing is heavily oriented towards semantic considerations. Case-frame parsers can cope with "ungrammatical" but meaningful sentences such as:

John the pumpkin ate.

Furthermore, terse expressions can be understood:

Print file1 printer2.

The semantics of *John*, *Pumpkin*, *Ate*, *Print*, *File1* and *Printer2* supply the case information that syntactic cues such as prepositions and word-order redundantly provide.

Case-frame parsing is usually associated with Schank's theory of Conceptual Dependency [63]. CD theory was the first to question the necessity of a grammar that formally distinguishes between autonomous levels of syntax, semantics, etc. Schank's main objection to traditional grammar-based natural language processing is that grammars traditionally emphasize syntax, whereas his thesis is that semantics should guide the parsing process. (We gloss over the fact that CD actually deals with "conceptual" cases, not "semantic" ones.)

There are problems with the hypothesis that language understanding consists solely of associating cases with verbs, however. Fillmore himself substantially tempered his espousal of case-grammars (and in fact repudiated his use of the term [27]). Syntactic complexities of natural language do not lend themselves to analyses in terms of verbs and cases, and natural language interfaces based on case-frame parsing are limited in their coverage of syntax.

There are advantages to incorporating case information in the parsing process. However, case-frames by themselves are not a sufficient formalism for all the (especially syntactic) complexities of natural language processing. One way to partially overcome the poor syntactic coverage of purely case-based systems is to integrate case-frames with a pattern-matching facility [1, 36].

As we said at the beginning of this chapter, this discussion by no means exhausts all the approaches that have been tried, nor even does it provide a complete list of advantages and disadvantages of the approaches considered. In the next chapter we will say some more about these and other approaches.

Chapter 3
A New Approach

Earlier, we claimed that a natural language interface for computer-aided design demands an approach of greater generality and power than previous approaches. The generality and power of our approach stems from the identification of two issues as being essential to the design of successful natural language interfaces for complex real-world domains: the degrees of flexibility and parallelism. In our discussion of these issues, we attempt to demonstrate their neglect in previous work and their importance, and we describe and exemplify their implementation in Cleopatra.

The flexibility and parallelism of Cleopatra complements and significantly extends what is in essence a lexically-driven case-frame parser. As we saw in the last chapter, a case-frame parser analyzes a sentence in terms of constituents (in particular the *cases*), which have some semantic connotations. (In traditional syntactic grammars, on the other hand, the constituents are purely syntactic abstractions.) We refer to Cleopatra as "lexically-driven" since each word in the input sentence invokes procedures that direct the parsing process. Conceptually, there is no higher-level procedure that reads each word and matches it against a pattern or rule under consideration.

3.1. Flexibility

There are several aspects of Cleopatra's flexibility, the two major ones being the flexibility of framing complex constraints on case-frame-to-verb-frame attachments, and the flexibility of specifying arbitrary and idiosyncratic actions to guide the parsing process. This section elaborates on the former; we will discuss the latter when we discuss the architecture of Cleopatra in the next chapter.

Before describing how constraints are represented in Cleopatra, let us examine why semantic-feature-based systems are inadequate in this respect.

3.1.1. Two Arguments Against Semantic Features

We believe that constraints on grammaticality and meaningfulness are much more complex than generally realized, especially within the artificial intelligence community. For a concrete example, let us look at the mechanism of "semantic features." Many traditional approaches to natural language understanding make use of semantic features to encode constraints on, typically, the grammatical relations (subject, object, etc.) of verbs. (These constraints are called "selectional restrictions.") In semantic grammars, this use is implicit; Conceptual Dependency parsers test the semantic features of prospective participants in ACT's (the CD equivalent of verbs); and most linguistic theories propose semantic features for lexical semantics.[6]

---

[6] In fact, selectional restrictions is not a topic of much active interest in linguistics today—perhaps it is considered a semantic issue by syntacticians, since it deals with information about meaning, yet relegated to syntax by semanticists, whose main concern is with semantic interpretation.

There are a couple of deficiencies of semantic-feature-based systems that demonstrate the importance of flexibility in the computational understanding of natural language.

1. As originally conceived [30], semantic features were no more than a hierarchical representation of unattributed values. Such a theory would postulate equivalence in terms of mental encoding for properties as diverse as *animate*, *edible*, and *transparent*, in order to accept a sentence such as the following:

   John saw the man having a hamburger through the window.[7]

   However, such a scheme is psychologically and linguistically quite inadequate. In later versions of semantic theory [44, 5], semantic features were represented as attributes and values. (Katz [44] represented only verbs this way.)

   It is easy to demonstrate that a catalog of semantic features is insufficient for the representation of semantic information. Consider the question:

   Is virtue edible?

   and two possible answers:

   No!

---

[7]The lexicon would list *animate* as a property of *John* and *man*, *edible* as a property of *hamburger*, and *transparent* as a property of *window*. This information, as well as such information as "the subject of *see* must be *animate*," "the subject and object of *have*, in one sense of the word, must be *animate* and *edible* respectively," "the object of the preposition *through*, in one sense of the word, must be *transparent*," would be employed to judge this sentence grammatical, on one of its many superficially possible readings.

S10. No, virtue is not a physical object.

No system that relied solely on the semantic features of individual lexical items (as sketched in Footnote 7) could come up with the latter answer. On the other hand, if the parser had recourse to a global hierarchical *network* of semantic features with labelled links, *(S10)* would be readily forthcoming.[8]

In the world of AI, there has been work on using semantic networks for knowledge representation, but this has never been tied in with work on natural language processing. Even systems constructed with the explicit goal of modelling psychological reality, such as Schank's [63], do not seem to have noticed the need for a semantic network component.

2. Semantic features are used for checking constraints on attachments; in particular, they are used for checking constraints a verb may impose on the constituents that can fill its case-roles. For the verb *eat*, such constraints could be: "The agent must have the feature *animate*," and "The object must have the feature *edible*." Note that these constraints are independent of each other. In fact, in most linguistics and AI work, there seems to be an implicit assumption that independent constraints are sufficient. This assumption is unjustified, as readily demonstrated:

   S11. John is a prince.

   *John is a princess.

   Fido has four paws.

---

[8]Go up the network from "edible" via IS-A's until a node that dominates "virtue" is reached. The daughter of this node that also dominates "edible" would be "physob".

*John has four paws.

The boa swallowed the cow.

*John swallowed the cow.

John married Joan.

*John married Bill.[9]

The truck hit the car on the fender.

*The truck hit the car in the solar plexus.

The ball caught John on the head.

S12. *The ball caught John on the left headlight.

These interdependencies are not confined to copulative verbs, or to nuclear constituents[10].

CD parsers, incidentally, seem to have the power to deal with such sentences. However, there has been no explicit recognition of the importance of such an ability in the CD literature and it would be surprising if CD parsers could readily handle such sentences in general. In fact PHRAN [1], which is a parser in the CD tradition, cannot make these discriminations.

To the best of our knowledge, there is no mention of such interdependencies in the literature. The closest reference is in

---

[9]Of course, the reading that is intended here is not that "John, in his capacity of priest, married Bill to someone."

[10]We follow Lyons' [50] use of "nuclear" and "extranuclear" constituents to refer to required and optional "cases."

[14], but Chomsky's concern there is with "syntactic features," not semantic ones. On page 119, Chomsky considers the deviance of the sentence:

> *His decision to resign his commission commanded the platoon.

The problem here is that both the subject, and the object of this sentence can be the subject and the object (individually) of the verb *command* in other contexts:

> His decision to resign his commission commanded our respect.
>
> He commanded the platoon.

Chomsky's tentative solution is to subcategorize a verb such as *command* as allowing an animate subject along with an animate object, or an abstract subject along with an abstract object. Such a scheme will not work for all the sentences given above.[11]

This discussion should have made clear that natural language understanding requires more knowledge about semantics than can be expressed by semantic features alone, and that simple, independent encoding of constraints on the basis of semantic features is not a

---

[11]On page 161 Chomsky discusses a similar set of sentences—for example, *The finger has a cut* and **The cut has a finger*. He concludes with the following paragraph:

> Once again, we can do no more here than indicate problems and stress the fact that there are many unanswered questions of principle that might very well affect the formulation of even those parts of the theory of grammar that seem reasonably well established.

sufficiently powerful mechanism for formulating selectional restrictions. Further research is needed for an adequate theoretical treatment of the issues outlined above; in particular, there is little agreement on approaches to knowledge representation. Pending such a theoretical treatment, it seems logical to retain as much flexibility as possible.

3.1.2. The Representation of Constraints in Cleopatra

In Cleopatra, we avoid any notion of a grammar implemented in a constrained formalism; constraints on grammaticality (such as what nominals a verb can have as its subject in a sentence) are not expressed through restrictive rules. Instead, such constraints are expressed, often implicitly, in the procedures and data structures that are invoked as specific words are processed. Even when explicit, constraints are in the form of arbitrary code (Lisp lambda bodies), and can therefore be arbitrary. Thus Cleopatra's formalism for encoding constraints allows us a high degree of flexibility.

There are in fact two separate sets of constraints associated with each verb in Cleopatra's vocabulary. One of these tests prospective case-fillers individually, without examining the other case-fillers, while the other tests collections of prospective case-fillers. These latter tests allow the encoding of the kinds of constraints that are needed for accepting or rejecting sentences such as *(S11) - (S12)*.

For example, here are the individual constraints on case-fillers for the verb *be* (Cleopatra incorporates restrictions imposed by the domain of circuit-simulation post-processing, of course, and the examples we present are not meant to be general for unrestricted English):

```
Subject:
   (lambda (x)
           (or (is-feature x 'quantity)
               (is-pos x 'existential-there))
        ; The subject must be a quantity (a
        ; number, a voltage , etc.) or the word
        ; "there" in its existential sense.

Predicate:
   (lambda (x) t)
        ; A null constraint.
```

The constraints are in the form of Lisp lambda-bodies, procedural bodies in which the variable (x here) is *bound* to some value before the expressions are evaluated. In this case, of course, x will be bound to a case-frame.[12] Only the constraints on the nuclear cases are associated with the verb. The individual constraints for the fillers of the extranuclear cases (such as the *locative* and the *temporal*) are to be found on the prospective case-fillers themselves.

Next, here are the "interdependencies" for the verb *be*:

---

[12]The effect of executing the *subject* case-filler constraint, with the variable *cf* representing a case-frame that is a candidate filler, would be equivalent to the Lisp expression *(or (is-feature cf 'quantity) (is-pos cf 'existential-there))*. This expression returns *t* (for *true*) if *cf* has *quantity* listed as one of its *features*, or if *cf* has *existential-there* listed as its *part-of-speech*; otherwise the expression returns *nil*.

```
Subject, Locative:
   (lambda (s l)
          (or (not (is-feature l 'node-id))
              (is-feature s 'function-noun)))
        ; The locative can be a node-identifier
        ; only if the subject is a function-noun
        ; (such as "voltage").

Subject, Predicate:
   (lambda (s p)
          (or (not (is-pos s 'existential-there))
              (not (is-type p 'comparative))))
        ; The existential "there" cannot be the
        ; subject of a comparative construction.

Predicate, Comparand:
   (special)
   (lambda (p c)
          (eq (not (not c))
              (is-type p 'comparative)))
        ; A comparand case (e.g. "than 3 volts")
        ; can be present if and only if the the
        ; predicate is a comparative ("greater").
```

The *special* symbol in the last constraint indicates that this constraint tests the presence or absence of a case-filler. Hence it is applied only when the verb-frame is being "closed" (i.e. when further case-frames cannot be attached to the verb-frame). The other constraints are applied as soon as all the case-roles mentioned are instantiated (and never applied if one or more of the case-roles are never instantiated).

As the above example shows, not only can we test the presence or absence of case-fillers, but their parts-of-speech ("pos"), their syntactic "types," and their "features," which can be semantic or syntactic. In fact, we can invoke any arbitrary function when evaluating a constraint.

In addition to the flexibility afforded by allowing arbitrary constraints, there is a different kind of flexibility that pertains to the "goodness-of-fit" of the constraints. This is useful, in concert with the confidence-levels described in the following section, for handling conjunctions, ellipses (incomplete sentences), and anaphora (referring expressions).

3.2. Parallelism, and Confidence Levels

3.2.1. Parallelism

The need for parallelism has to do with the phenomenon of ambiguity. All languages exhibit ambiguity at all levels, from the phoneme to discourse. In fact, ambiguity allows the relatively efficient encoding of linguistic content—if, for example, there were no ambiguous structures in a language, the size of the grammar would be prohibitively large (and perhaps even infinite[13]), but most of the constructions would be rarely used. Ambiguity is more than just "a useful conservation of linguistic resources" [34;p.63]; it is an essential and an inevitable linguistic phenomenon.

Nevertheless, many natural language interfaces do not attempt to handle ambiguity. Since most previous interfaces have been limited to

---

[13]The sentences *John saw the girl in April, John saw the girl who lived in the city in April, John saw the girl who lived in the city that elected a mayor in April,* can be extended indefinitely. The trailing prepositional phrase (*in April*) can be a constituent of any clause. If the grammar did not allow such syntactic ambiguities, it would need some syntactic device that specified which of the indefinitely many prior verbs the prepositional phrase was associated with.

narrow domains, this failing has not been fatal to the success of these interfaces. In fact, two of the most widely known natural language interfaces, LADDER [38] and PLANES [73], could not handle ambiguous sentences. Both these interfaces utilize augmented transition networks for parsing, and ATN's are not well-suited for dealing with ambiguity.

In a more general vein, there has even been some research to demonstrate that languages can be parsed deterministically [51]. (In other words, that the parsing of a sentence does not require the construction of any structure that eventually has to be undone or discarded. A parallel parsing strategy, on the other hand, would construct structures that would later be discarded.) However, the computational implementation of this work, a parser called PARSIFAL, could not handle lexical ambiguity (multiple meanings of a word), prepositional phrase attachment (a rich source of ambiguity, as we saw above), or conjunctions (another construction that exhibits ambiguity) [77;p.410]. Nor was this work just a theoretical exploration; at least two natural language understanding systems use a PARSIFAL-like parser [79, 49].

There is a further remark about PARSIFAL that we would like to make. PARSIFAL's garden-path handling[14] was proclaimed as strong evidence for the determinism hypothesis (the hypothesis that language can be parsed deterministically). However, once a particular garden-path sentence has been heard and explicated, subsequent utterances of it do not cause hearers to garden-path. On first reading, *The toy rocks near*

---

[14]A *garden-path* sentence leads the hearer "down the garden path." The initial portion of the sentence sets up strong expectations for the remaining portion, but these expectations are violated. Examples: *The prime number few*, *The horse raced past the barn fell.*

the child quietly requires some "mental backtracking" to process. Subsequently, neither this sentence nor *The toy rocks near the child are pink* causes any perplexity. This phenomenon does not accord with the determinism hypothesis. (For another, related criticism of PARSIFAL, see [52].)

Given that languages are ambiguous and that natural language interfaces must deal with ambiguity, there are two mechanisms which are available to the interface builder: Ambiguity can be handled either through parallelism, in which case the parser works on all possible interpretations as each word is encountered, or through some form or other of backtracking, in which case the parser fully explores a particular interpretation before going back and starting on another. Because of its depth-first nature, however, backtracking is better suited for coming up with a single valid parse. ATN's usually employ backtracking, and it is therefore small wonder that ATN-based parsers are often deficient when it comes to the handling of ambiguity.

Cleopatra utilizes parallelism for handling ambiguity. Structures that are assigned to portions of the input during processing are called *parse-states*. There can be many such competing structures at any point in the processing. During the processing of a word, as many new parse-states are instantiated as there are possible interpretations (that Cleopatra knows about) of the word in the context of the previous words of the sentence. The different lexical senses of the word (for example, the word *output* used as a verb and as a noun), and the different structures the word can help constitute (for example, *output* as in *the output* and in *the output voltage*), will result in separate parse-states. As additional words in the sentence are read, some of these parse-states are recognized to be invalid and are terminated.

We should perhaps remark that Cleopatra's parallelism has nothing in common with "massively parallel" or "connectionist" approaches to language processing [17, 74]. Both the cited papers are concerned mainly with word-sense disambiguation, which is a difficult problem in a general natural language understanding system, but not in our domain-restricted case.

3.2.2. Confidence-Levels

There is nothing extraordinary about a parsing process that produces all possible parses; many natural language interfaces are similar to Cleopatra in this respect [37, 48, 60, 67], although it is usually not indicated in their published descriptions whether these systems use parallelism or backtracking internally.

In Cleopatra, however, this parallelism is supplemented with a notion of *confidence-levels* for parse-states. The confidence-level indicates numerically the likelihood that the parse-state is on the right track—in other words, the likelihood that the eventual best parse will be a descendant of this parse-state. Confidence-levels are dynamic; they can change from parse-state to parse-state. The relative frequencies of occurrence of different senses of a word, the likelihood of particular structures, and the correspondence of conjuncts, are some of the factors that can be taken into account in the calculation and updating of confidence-levels. These confidence-level factors might also eventually allow Cleopatra to be "tuned" for individual users.

Though parallelism and backtracking are often thought of as formally equivalent, there is a sense in which parallelism with confidence-levels is more powerful than backtracking with confidence-levels: A parser built on the former principle allows the mutual inhibition of competing parses, a parser built on the latter principle does not. Cleopatra at present does not have a mutual-inhibition feature, but one could prove useful as Cleopatra's domain widens, and a better handling of ambiguity becomes imperative.

Cleopatra does not prohibit non-breadth-first parsing strategies. (In this context, "breadth-first" implies "fully parallel.") If at any point too many parse-states are in contention, the parse-states with the lower confidence-levels could be suspended. Since each parse-state contains the portion of the input that has still to be processed, this suspension can be temporary. (At present Cleopatra's parsing strategy is exclusively breadth-first; the details of this suggested best-first strategy have not been implemented.)

Measures similar to confidence-levels have been used in other fields in artificial intelligence (in expert systems [66, 23, 20] and in a speech-understanding system [24], for example). Just recently, an "experimental" natural language interface, MULTIPAR, has been described that uses *tolerance levels* [25]. Tolerance levels in MULTIPAR, however, are measures of grammatical deviance; they cannot be used to disambiguate multiple grammatically correct interpretations.

Disambiguating sentences automatically requires a device, such as Cleopatra's confidence-levels, that can be used to rate possible interpretations. Some systems incorporate heuristics which are invoked when a sentence is recognized as ambiguous. In fact, Cleopatra in an earlier version used such a heuristic ("Select the parse with the most attachments to the main verb."). Confidence-levels are a more principled and less *ad hoc* mechanism for disambiguation.

3.2.3. Updating Confidence-Levels

Let us now discuss the updating of confidence-levels. There are two different procedures for updating that we will consider:

1. Weighted-average updating

2. Additive updating

By weighted-average updating we mean that, in order to arrive at the new confidence-level, each new updating factor is multipled by a weight and added to the current confidence-level also multiplied by some weight, and the resulting sum is divided by the sum of the weights.

By additive updating we mean that each new updating factor is added to or subtracted from the current confidence-level to give the new confidence-level.

Though intuitively the first procedure seems more reasonable, it has a couple of severe disadvantages for our purposes:

- In a weighted-average update, a division (or a multiplication by a less than unity weight) has to be done in order to keep the confidence-levels within reasonable bounds. However, this introduces a degradation of precision. Differences between competing parses can get diluted as the parse progresses. This can pose problems, especially with long sentences. In additive updating, on the other hand, even small differences are maintained.

- Unlike additive updating, weighted-average updating is sensitive to the ordering of the updates. Cleopatra does not always invoke factors in the same order. For example, consider the sentence:

What is the voltage at n1?

We presume that this sentence has two interpretations: one in which *at n1* is predicated of *the voltage*, and the other in which it is predicated of the verb. In the first case Cleopatra attaches *at n1* to *the voltage* before it attaches *the voltage* to the verb. In the second case, *the voltage* is attached to the verb before *at n1*. Assuming that the update-factors for the two attachments of *the voltage* are identical and that the update-factors for the two attachments of *at n1* are also identical (but different from the first identity), the final confidence-levels for the two interpretations will be different if calculated using a weighted-average scheme. This is true even if all the weights are identical!

For these reasons we use a variant of an additive scheme for the updating of confidence-levels. In Cleopatra, a confidence-level is usually never increased. Whenever a parse-state is instantiated that represents a somewhat uncommon construction, or a less than perfect match between conjuncts or between a constituent and its substitute in an ellipsis, indeed whenever there is some reason to suspect that the parse-state might not lead to the eventual best parse, the confidence-level is decremented by some (variable) amount. Otherwise, no change is made to the confidence-level.

Chapter 4
The Parsing Process

In the last chapter, we cursorily outlined the representational flexibility and the highly-parallel operation of Cleopatra's parser. In this chapter we examine the parsing process in depth. Since some understanding of parse-states is a prerequisite for understanding the parsing process, we begin with a discussion of parse-states.

The parsing process builds a tree of partial parses as it progresses. Each node of this tree is a partial parse called a parse-state. (The terminal nodes, which represent completed parses, are also called parse-states.) Cleopatra parses sentences left-to-right, and therefore each parse-state represents an analysis of the portion of the sentence beginning with the first morpheme[15] in the sentence and ending with the last morpheme read before that parse-state was instantiated. A parse-state consists of seven variables:

state-id	A unique identifier for the parse-state.
parent-id	The ****state-id**** of the parent parse-state.

---

[15] *Morpheme* is the linguistic term for the smallest unit of meaning. A word can be composed of multiple morphemes. Example: the word *voltages* has two morphemes: the *voltage* morpheme, and the *plural* morpheme, realized as the *-s* suffix in this case.

sconf The confidence-level of the parse-state.

rem The remaining words in the input (i.e. the words that have yet to be processed). The presence of this variable would allow running Cleopatra in non-breadth-first fashion, as we mentioned in the last chapter.

frames A list of the verb-frames that have been instantiated in the parse-state. There is one verb-frame on **frames** for each verb in the portion of the sentence represented by the parse-state. (We will elaborate on this later, but for the present a verb-frame can be considered to represent a verb, a noun-frame a noun, and so on.)

buff A list of determiner-frames, adjective-frames, noun-frames, etc., that have not been composed into higher-level constituents. Elements on **buff** are ultimately combined to form case-frames which also reside on **buff** temporarily, but which ultimately fill case-roles of verb-frames on **frames**.

vbuff Similar to **buff**, but concerned with "verbal" information. **Vbuff** contains information about tense, aspect, etc., as well as adverbs, for all verbs that have not themselves been seen until this parse-state. (Verbal information, if it is not in the form of an adverb, always precedes the verb it applies to.) **Vbuff** indicates clause-boundaries. As soon as a verb is encountered, all the items on **vbuff** until (and including) the last clause-boundary marker are deleted. Since Cleopatra is not very sophisticated about auxiliaries or adverbs[16], **vbuff** is not used extensively. Both **buff** and **vbuff** act somewhat like last-in first-out stacks. Only the most recent element on either of these variables is immediately accessible.

Although confidence-levels are an essential feature of Cleopatra's approach, we will ignore their role in the parsing process throughout this chapter, and for most of the next. In the last section of the next chapter we will illustrate in some detail how confidence-levels are affected as the parse progresses.

4.1. Lexical Entries

Cleopatra's parser is lexically-driven. Each word that is in Cleopatra's vocabulary has a *lexical procedure* associated with it.[17] As each word of the input is read, its lexical procedure is executed. The lexical procedure returns a *lexical entry*, which is a list of lists of procedures. Each list of procedures constitutes a sense of the word, and is executed sequentially. The lexical entry constitutes all the senses of the word Cleopatra knows

---

[16]Note, however, that a lexically-driven approach such as Cleopatra's is better suited for processing adverbs than a pattern-matching or a rule-based approach. (The word-order constraints on adverbs are few and irregular. *Slowly, John walked home*, *John slowly walked home*, and *John walked home slowly*, are all acceptable.) Note also that the position of an adverb can affect meaning: *John drinks coffee in the morning frequently* can mean that John drinks many cups of coffee each morning, whereas *Frequently John drinks coffee in the morning* cannot. Such a distinction could also be better captured in Cleopatra than in other, less-powerful natural language interfaces.

[17]Numbers and node-identifiers have one generic lexical procedure each, which takes the number or the node-identifier as an argument.

about. (Thus lexical ambiguity is handled in the lexical entry.) The different senses can, for our purposes, be considered to be executed in parallel.

The procedures within a list of procedures are organized in pairs; there can be as many pairs as there are morphemes in the sense represented by that list of procedures. The first procedure in each pair is called a *dictionary procedure*, the second an *integration procedure*.

For example, here is the lexical entry for the word *voltage*:

```
(((*voltage1) (generic-noun-1)))
```

Voltage has only one sense, and only one morpheme in that sense. The name of the dictionary procedure is **voltage1*, and the name of the integration procedure is *generic-noun-1*.

The verb *equals* also has only one sense, but it has two morphemes in that sense: the present-tense morpheme and the root-verb morpheme. (Cleopatra does not know about "person" and "number" as yet.) The lexical entry for *equals* is:[18]

```
(((*pres) (tns equal)
  (*equal2) (generic-verbs-1)))
```

**Pres* and *tns* are the dictionary and integration procedures for the present-tense morpheme, and **equal2* and *generic-verbs-1* are the dictionary and integration procedures for the root-verb morpheme. *Tns* is the only integration procedure that takes an argument. The argument is the name of the verb if the tense carrier is a verb, and *nil* if the tense carrier is an auxiliary element.

---

[18]No morphological analysis is attempted presently.

For a last example, here is the lexical entry for *equal*:

```
(((*equal1) (generic-comp-case-1))
 ((*pres2) (tns equal)
  (*equal2) (generic-verbs-1)))
```

Equal has two senses, composed of one and two morphemes respectively. The first sense is the one involved in comparative sentences:

Is the voltage at n1 equal to 2 volts?

In this sense *equal* is treated as the predicate of the verb *be*.

The second sense is the verbal one, with a tense morpheme and a root-verb morpheme. The dictionary procedure for the tense morpheme for *equal* (**pres2*) differs from the dictionary procedure for the tense morpheme for *equals* (**pres*) only in that the former includes a feature that allows a previous tense morpheme to over-ride the tense information. For example, the word *equal* contributes the present-tense information in a sentence such as *The voltages at n1 and n2 equal 2 volts*, but does not contribute this information in a sentence such as *When does the voltage at n1 equal 2 volts?* (Note that *equals* cannot be used in the latter context.)

Actually, all verbs in root form in English (except the verb *be*) are ambiguous. They can be morphologically analyzed as *<first-person-present-tense>* + *<root-verb>*, and also as just *<root-verb>*. Rather than have an extra entry in the lexical procedure for each verb in root form, we effectively let the integration procedure for tense be a null procedure when the verb is in root form and tense information has already been encountered (i.e. when tense information is already present on **vbuff**).

4.2. Dictionary Entries

Dictionary procedures have *dictionary entries* associated with them. A dictionary entry for a morpheme represents declarative knowledge about the morpheme. The dictionary entry for a noun, for example, will indicate its (semantic and syntactic) features, the case-roles it can fill, the adjectives and determiners that modify it, etc. Here we will examine one dictionary entry each for a noun and a verb.

We think of dictionary entries as *frames*. Thus we will refer to dictionary entries for nouns as *noun-frames*, for verbs as *verb-frames*, and so on. The attributes of frames are called *slots*, and their values are called *slot-values*. Although this terminology is analogous to the terminology used with frames in other AI work, our frames lack the sophistication of most of these other frames. In particular, we do not incorporate procedural attachment, demons, or inheritance. Thus, the use of frames serves principally to rationalize the organization of information in the lexical knowledge base.

First, here is the noun-frame for the noun *voltage* (alternatively, the dictionary entry for the dictionary procedure **voltage1*):

```
{
 [id: c00001]
 [pos: n]
 [value: voltage]
 [type: ]
 [x-v: ]
 [cases-for:
    (subj (lambda (x (is-feature x 'v-class1))
          before-v)
    (pred (lambda (x) t) after-v)
```

```
    (obj (lambda (x) (is-feature x 'v-class1))
         after-v)
    (comparand (lambda (x) (is-feature x 'v-class1))
         after-v)]
  [connections: ]
  [attachments: ]
  [features: function-noun count-n prefix-f quantity]
  [lf: !voltage!]
  [d-proc: *voltage1]
}
```

Before we discuss the slots individually, we should point out that more slots can be added to frames if the need arises during the parsing process. Thus, although there are no slots present for the association of adjectives or units (*volts*, *ns*, etc.) with a noun-frame, when an adjective or a unit is recognized as applying to a noun, an *adj:* slot or a *units:* slot is appended to the noun-frame.

The *id:* slot-value is a unique identifier for this frame. The *pos:* slot indicates the part-of-speech, which in this case is a noun (denoted by the letter *n*). When this noun-frame eventually forms a prospective case-filler (perhaps in combination with other frames) this slot-value will be changed to *case*. The *type:* slot will then indicate whether the case is an *np* (noun-phrase) or a *pp* (prepositional-phrase). The *type:* slot also indicates if the case-frame is a relative-pronoun. The *value:* slot indicates the word the frame represents. The slot-value for the *x-v:* slot indicates whether this frame was encountered before the verb or after the verb. (Verb-frames also have an *x-v:* slot, and its interpretation is different there, as we shall see.)

The *cases-for:* slot lists all the case-roles a noun-frame can fill (when the noun-frame becomes a case-frame of which the noun-frame represents the main, or "head," noun). Associated with each case-role are the constraints that a verb has to satisfy before the case-frame can fill that case-role of the verb.[19] For example, the first constraint states that *voltage* can fill the *subject* case-role of a verb-frame if the verb-frame has *v-class1* on its *features:* slot. The *before-v* and *after-v* symbols indicate whether that case occurs before or after the verb in a "normal" declarative sentence. This is usually ignored for prepositional phrases, and can also be ignored or manipulated for constructions such as passives, frontings, etc. The *comparand* case-role, incidentally, is used in comparative constructions. For example, we call *than 3 volts* the comparand case in *Is the voltage at n1 greater than 3 volts?*

A description of the function of the *connections:* slot is best initiated by an example. Assume that the input sentence contains an adjective (represented by an adjective-frame) that modifies a noun. First, a "surrogate" id is generated for the adjective-frame. This id is then used in place of the real id in the noun-frame. Thus if the surrogate id is *x00003*, the *adj:* slot of the noun-frame would read *[adj: x00003]*. This surrogate id is related to the real id in the *connections:* slot. The *connections:* slot consists of a list of pairs (implemented as dotted pairs in Lisp), the first element of each being a surrogate-id, the second the associated real id. In our example, if the (real) id of the adjective-frame is *a00002*, the *connections:* slot of the noun-frame would read *[connections: (x00003 . a00002)]*. All references to other frames within a frame are through surrogate-id's. When the actual referent frames need to be accessed, the surrogate id's are used as keys on the *connections:* slot-value.

Use of surrogate-id's is obviously a round-about way of effecting

---

[19] Recall that the verb-frame also lists the constraints on its nuclear cases. Distributed constraints facilitate modifications and extensions.

connections. There is, however, justification for it. Cleopatra's parsing strategy is highly parallel. One parse-state will often lead to multiple parse-states. When that happens, copies need to be made of some frames. Since the new parse-states differ from each other, the copies of particular frames will also differ. Frames which referred to the original copy of a frame will need to be updated by substituting the new id (for the new copy) in place of the old id (for the original copy). By keeping all the real id's on the *connections:* slot alone, we avoid having to search all the other slots for the old real id. The surrogate id's never change; the same surrogate id, when used after an update, will now access a different frame.

In the preceding example, we considered the case of an adjective modifying a noun. Similarly, when a case-filler is associated with a verb, or an adverb is associated with a verb, the real id for, respectively, the case-frame or the adverb-frame, is only indicated on the *connections:* slot of the verb-frame. All references to the case-frame or the adverb-frame in the other slots of the verb-frame are through surrogate id's.

The reader may have generalized from the above examples that it is always the "higher-level" constituent that refers to "lower-level" constituents on its *connections:* slot. The *connections:* slot of an adjective-frame, for example, does not reference the noun-frame that the adjective-frame modifies. This generalization, though in any case not prescriptive, is invalid in one instance: It is the relative pronoun that refers to the head of a relative clause, and not vice versa.

References to frames are not only via the *connections:* slot. In fact, for every reference made by frame A, via its *connections:* slot, to frame B, there is an opposite reference made by frame B, via its *attachments:* slot, to frame A. There are no surrogate id's for the *attachments:* slots, and when a frame reference via the *attachments:* slot is modified, its new id is appended to the *attachments:* slot without deleting the original id. The *attachments:* slot is used only in the updating process, to access the frames which refer to a (now modified) frame through their *connections:* slots. For example, if for some reason some slot-value of an adjective-frame is changed, and if the adjective-frame has already been attached to a noun-frame, then the *attachments:* slot of the adjective-frame (which will list the real id of the noun-frame), can be used to access the noun-frame, and the *connections:* slot of the noun-frame can then be updated. (A modification of a frame is not done to the original frame, but to a copy of it, which has a different id.)

The *features:* slot is used for semantic and syntactic features whose presence or absence may be tested in constraints, in integration procedures, or in the semantic interpretation procedure. Features are non-decomposable; they are not attribute-value pairs, for instance. The *lf:* slot lists the name of the function that is invoked for the semantic interpretation of this frame, after the parsing process has successfully terminated. The semantic interpretation process is discussed in Chapter 7.

Before discussing the *d-proc:* slot, we need to digress briefly and examine the process by which prepositions (called *case-markers* in the case-frame parsing terminology) influence the case-roles a case-frame can fill.

As we saw above, the *cases-for:* slot lists all the possible case-roles a noun-frame can fill (after it helps form a case-frame of which it is the head-noun). However, prepositions can disallow some of these case-roles as possibilities. For example, the noun-phrase *the voltage at n1* can be used to fill any of the four case-roles (*subj, pred, obj, comparand*), though the *comparand* case-role is only acceptable (and marginally at that) as a terse form: *When is the voltage at n1 greater the voltage at n2?*

However, if the preposition *than* appears before *the voltage at n1*, then only the *comparand* case-role is a possibility; the prepositional-phrase *than the voltage at n1* cannot be the subject, the predicate, or the object of a verb. The case-roles that a noun can fill when it is the object of a preposition are listed on the *marker-for:* slot of the preposition-frame representing that preposition. The *marker-for:* slot also indicates the constraints on the associated noun-frame for each case-role the preposition-noun compound can possibly fill. Thus, for the preposition *than*, the *marker-for:* slot is:

```
[marker-for:
    (comparand
       (lambda (x) (is-feature x 'quantity)))]
```

This slot-value says that a noun-frame can be the object of the preposition *than* as a possible case-filler for the *comparand* case-role if the noun-frame has *quantity* on its *features:* slot-value. When a noun is recognized as the object of a preposition, the *marker-for:* slot is used to come up with a new set of possible case-roles. These case-roles are a subset of the case-roles indicated in the *cases-for:* slot of the noun-frame, and a subset of the case-roles indicated in this *marker-for:* slot. All the case-roles on the *cases-for:* slot that are not sanctioned by the *marker-for:* slot are deleted from the *cases-for:* slot. In this process, the information about which case-roles the noun-frame could fill (if it was not the object of that preposition) is lost.

There is one construction that requires that the original case-roles of a noun phrase (with which a preceding preposition has been associated) be retrieved. This is the relative clause construction. Cleopatra attaches a preposition to a following (simple) noun phrase before checking to see whether that noun phrase is the head of a relative clause. If such is indeed the case, then, when the relative clause is instantiated, the relative clause head does not list all the case-roles that the relative pronoun can fill.[20]

The *d-proc:* slot-value (to end our digression) is the name of the dictionary procedure for the morpheme. The dictionary procedure is executed to get the original dictionary entry, and it is the *cases-for:* slot from this dictionary entry that is copied onto the relative pronoun frame. (Most other slot-values for the relative pronoun frame are inherited on demand from the relative clause head.) In general, the *d-proc:* slot allows the recovery of information originally in the dictionary entry which subsequent processing has deleted or modified.

(There is a better way of ensuring that a relative pronoun has the right constraints associated with it: Instead of deleting the entry for a particular case-role from the *cases-for:* slot, Cleopatra could append a special symbol to that entry. The presence of that symbol could indicate to the case-filling procedures that that case-role is not a possibility for the case-frame. The relative-clause instantiating procedures, on the other hand, would ignore the symbol when copying the *cases-for:* slot from the head to the pronoun frame.)

---

[20]Cleopatra does not check if a noun-phrase with a preceding preposition is immediately followed by the word *and* before attaching the preposition to the noun-phrase either. Thus Cleopatra would parse the phrase *In France and Italy* as *((in France) and (Italy))* rather than as *(in ((France) and (Italy)))*, although the latter is clearly the correct analysis. Possible negative consequences of Cleopatra's analysis can, however, be averted by making the conjunction handling procedures more sophisticated.

That concludes our discussion of the dictionary entry for a noun-frame. Verb-frames and noun-frames have some slots in common, and other slots specific to one or the other. In discussing a verb-frame, we will only examine those slots which we have not encountered in the above discussion, or whose usage in verb-frames differs from that in noun-frames. Furthermore, we have already explained the interpretation of both the individual constraints (the *cases:* slot) and the inter-dependencies (the ***inter-constraints:*** slot) in the previous chapter. (The *p-locative* case-role-filler, incidentally, encodes information about *physical-location*; at present only nodes, which we think of as points in space, can fill the *p-locative* case-role.)

Here is the verb-frame for the verb *be* (more precisely, the dictionary entry for the root-verb morpheme):

```
{
 [id: v00001]
 [pos: v]
 [name: be]
 [tns: ]
 [mode: ]
 [x-v: ]
 [cases:
    (subj (lambda (x)
               (or (is-feature x 'quantity)
                   (is-pos x 'existential-there)))
          before-v)
    (pred (lambda (x) t) after-v)]
 [inter-constraints:
    ((subj p-locative)
     (lambda (s p)
            (or (not (is-feature p 'node-id))
                (is-feature s 'function-noun))))
    ((subj pred)
     (lambda (s p)
            (or (not (is-pos s 'existential-there))
```

```
                    (not (is-type p 'comparative)))))
    (special
     (pred comparand)
     (lambda (p c)
             (or (not c) (is-type p 'comparative)))))]
  [adv-constraints:
    ((comparand)
     (lambda (adv c) (or (not adv) c)))]
  [case-fills: ]
  [pending: ]
  [connections: ]
  [attachments: ]
  [status: open]
  [features: v-class1]
  [eval: !be-1!]
}
```

The *tns:* slot-value is the tense associated with the verb. The *mode:* slot indicates whether the verb is a main-verb or a subordinate clause verb. If the former, then the *mode:* slot indicates if the sentence is a yes-no question or a *wh*-question. If the latter, then it indicates whether the subordinate clause is a relative clause, or an object clause of one of the prepositions *before* and *after*. (These are the only types of subordinate clauses that Cleopatra handles currently.) The *mode:* slot is also used to indicate if the sentence is a *wh*-fronted sentence. The *x-v:* slot indicates whether the verb's integration procedure has been run or not. After the execution of the dictionary procedure, the integration procedure is executed. The *x-v:* slot-value is *before-v* while the integration procedure is running. Just before exiting the integration procedure, this slot-value is changed to *after-v*.

The *adv-constraints:* slot lists the constraints that must be satisfied before an adverb can be attached to a verb-frame. Cleopatra currently only allows the adverbs *ever*, *never*, and *always*, and the constraint says that an adverb can only modify the verb *be* if a *comparand* case is present (alternatively, only in a comparative construction).

Again, we digress (briefly) before explaining the *case-fills:* and *pending:* slots. When a case-frame is attached to a verb-frame, there are two possibilities: There may be only one possible case-role that the case-frame can fill, or there may be more than one. For example, the case-frame representing the prepositional phrase *than 3 volts* can only fill the *comparand* case-role, while the case-frame representing the prepositional phrase *at 5 ns* can fill either the temporal case-role or the predicate case-role (for the verb *be*). It is the *wh*-fronting construction that really demonstrates the potential ambiguity of case-role instantiation convincingly. In the following sentences, the portions of the sentences until the verb are identical, yet the initial noun-phrase (*what*) fills a different case-role in each:

What did John give the dog?

What did John give the croissant to?

What did John give the croissant to the dog for?

What did John give the croissant to the dog in?

What did John give the croissant to the dog on?

If a case-frame is present on **buff** when a verb is encountered, and if the case-frame is considered attachable to the verb, then Cleopatra will not leave it on **buff**, even if the case-role of the case-frame cannot be uniquely determined at that point.

If the case-role of a case-frame can be uniquely determined, the case-frame is placed on the *case-fills:* slot. If more than one case-roles are possible, the case-frame is placed on the *pending:* slot. The *case-fills:* and the *pending:* slots also list the unique case-role and the multiple case-roles (respectively) for a case-frame. Whenever a case-frame is attached whose case-role is unique, that case-role is deleted from the lists of prospective case-roles of all the case-frames on the *pending:* slot. If some case-frame is thereby left on the *pending:* slot with one prospective case-role, then that case-frame is instantiated as the filler of that case-role on the *case-fills:* slot. (This process is recursively repeated until there is no case-frame on *pending:* with just one possible case-role.)

Wh-frontings are handled in a slightly different way. Since a *wh*-fronted noun phrase can fill almost any case-role, its associated case-frame is placed on *pending:* not with a list of possible case-roles, but with a list of possible nuclear (or required) case-roles (which usually are not filled by prepositional phrases) along with a special character (an asterisk). Whenever a preposition is encountered after a *wh* case-frame has been placed on *pending:*, the *wh* case-frame is retrieved, its *cases-for:* slot is matched against the *marker-for:* slot of the preposition-frame, and the attachment of the resulting case-frame (now representing a prepositional phrase) is attempted afresh. Of course, the *wh* case-frame may not really be the object of this preposition, and so an alternative interpretation is also initiated, in which the preposition is treated normally (in most cases, simply placed on **buff**). When the verb-frame is ultimately closed to further attachments, the *pending:* slot is searched for a case-frame with an asterisk in its list of possible case-roles. If such a case-frame is found, the asterisk is deleted. If any (nuclear) case-role is left, then the fronted *wh* phrase is presumed not to be the object of a preposition, and the case-frame is instantiated as the filler of the nuclear case-role.

If a contradiction arises during this process (e.g. more than one case-frame ends up with the same case-role, or all the possible case-roles for a case-frame are deleted) then that parse-state is assumed incorrect. If on the other hand there are multiple possible case-roles for a case-frame on *pending:* when the verb-frame is closed, the first of these is taken.

The *eval:* slot lists the name of the function that is invoked for the semantic interpretation of this frame, after the parsing process has successfully terminated. (There is no real reason why the slot that serves the same function in case-frames is called *lf:*.)

4.3. Integration Procedures

We have just seen that a dictionary procedure has a dictionary entry that is associated with it and that represents information about a morpheme. The dictionary procedure assigns the dictionary entry to a global variable **tmp**. It is the task of the integration procedure to interpret **tmp** in the context of the current parse-state. As we said before, this context is limited to the (interpreted) string of morphemes prior to **tmp** in the sentence.

It may be that the morpheme is non-sensical in the current context, in which case the integration procedure should not spawn any new parse-states. On the other hand, it may be that the morpheme can be interpreted in multiple ways, in which case the integration procedure should spawn as many new parse-states as there are possible interpretations. (Structural ambiguity, then, is handled in integration procedures.) Of course, such ambiguity is often "transient." The broadening of context caused by just the next morpheme may be sufficient to invalidate some of these new parse-states.

Integration procedures are arbitrary Lisp functions. They are often generic to the part-of-speech, but they need not be—every morpheme could have its own integration procedure if so deemed necessary. This lack of structure and formalism in integration procedures, while further illustrating the flexibility inherent in Cleopatra, has an unfortunate consequence that only the process of writing this thesis has fully revealed: Describing particular integration procedures in English is a daunting task!

Nevertheless, we will attempt it, albeit at the expense of considerable fine detail. We will describe integration procedures for nouns and for tense information. Our descriptions will leave some holes, some of which will be filled in the next chapter.

Before describing the integration procedure for nouns, it will be helpful to examine how **buff** functions. Recall that **buff** contains nominal constituents: determiner-frames, adjective-frames, noun-frames, etc. These are combined to form case-frames. Case-frames eventually must fill case-roles in verb-frames. (Verb-frames reside on **frames**.) If the verb to which a case can be attached has not been read as yet (i.e. the verb is more to the right than the sequence of words which constitute the case in the input sentence), then the case-frame will be placed on **buff** for the time being. Even if its verb has preceded it, however, a case-frame is not attached to the verb-frame as soon as it is formed. If it were, then the case-frame could not be recognized as a conjunct, the first operand of an infix function, or a relative-clause head. (The procedures which initiate these constructions look only on **buff** for constituents, and when a case-frame is attached to a verb-frame it is removed from **buff**.)

Thus whenever a case-frame is formed, it is placed on **buff**. It is only when two contiguous elements on **buff** are both case-frames that the attachment of the first (earlier) case-frame to a verb-frame can be attempted. (Two contiguous case-frames can also signal a relative clause as in *The man John saw.* The integration procedure will instantiate a separate parse-state if such a relative clause construction is possible.) Of course, if no further words are left in the input sentence, case-frames on **buff** can be attached to verb-frames without any delay.

4.3.1. The integration procedure for nouns

At present, there is one integration procedure for nouns, called *generic-nouns-1*. When *generic-nouns-1* is invoked, **tmp** contains the dictionary entry for a noun. By "retrieving a *btop*" or "getting a new *btop*" in the following description, we mean that the most recent element on **buff** is removed from **buff** and assigned to the variable *btop*.

1. Retrieve a *btop*.

2. If *btop* is a noun, then process for noun-groups. (There are structural ambiguities associated with noun-groups that have to be considered. Though most of the code for noun-group handling is present in *generic-nouns-1*, the utility of noun-groups in Cleopatra's current domain is extremely limited. We will not describe how noun-groups could be handled in Cleopatra, except to say that we presume that noun-groups have a binary tree structure, and that in each pair of nouns, or noun-groups, the second element is the head. In any case, the noun-group processing would be done for each *btop* until a *btop* is retrieved that is not a noun.)

3. If *btop* is an adjective, then attach *btop* to **tmp**, get a new *btop* and repeat this step. (Again there are some structural ambiguities associated with noun-groups that are irrelevant here. We presume that *btop* actually modifies **tmp**. The adjective-noun attachment is done for each *btop* until a *btop* is retrieved that is not an adjective.)

4. If *btop* is an article, then attach *btop* to **tmp**, and get a new *btop*. (Here too there is a structural ambiguity associated with the noun group construction that we gloss over. There are separate procedures for attaching adjectives to nouns, for attaching articles to nouns, etc.)

5. If *btop* is a case-marker (a preposition), then attempt an attachment of it to **tmp**. If this attachment fails, then terminate the integration procedure. (The attachment could fail for either of two reasons: There is no case-role that the *cases-for:* slot of **tmp** and the *marker-for:* slot of *btop* have in common, or the constraints imposed by the *marker-for:* slot on the common cases are not satisfied.) If the attachment succeeds, then modify the *cases-for:* slot of **tmp** as described earlier (page 49), change the *pos:* slot-value of **tmp** from *n* to *case*, append *pp* (for *prepositional phrase*) to the *type:* slot-value, and get a new *btop*.

   Else if *btop* is not a case-marker, then change the *pos:* slot-value of **tmp** from *n* to *case*, and append *np* (for *noun phrase*) to the *type:* slot-value.

6. If *btop* is a conjunction or an infix arithmetic function, then place *btop* and **tmp** on **buff**, instantiate a new parse-state, and terminate the integration procedure. (**Tmp** could be the second conjunct or operand. However, it is not instantiated as such until Cleopatra makes sure that it is not the head of a relative clause or the *first* conjunct or operand of another conjunction or infix function.)

7. If the *type:* slot-value of **tmp** includes *np*, and *btop* has *case* on its *pos:* slot, *before-v* on its *x-v:* slot, and *wh* on its *features:* slot, then

   a. Add *wh-fronted* to the *features:* slot of *btop*. (Since **tmp** is a noun-phrase, it must be the subject. Usually, only the subject case occurs before the verb.

Since *btop* is also a case, its usual position must be post-verbal. Hence it is "fronted." The only non-subject noun-phrases that can occur before the verb are *wh* noun phrases such as *what, why, which node,* etc.)

b. Get the most recent clause-boundary-marker-frame from **vbuff** and assign it to the variable *vbtop*.

c. Add *wh-fronted* and *q* to the *mode:* slot of *vbtop*. (This clause is an interrogative one and it has a fronted *wh* phrase.)

d. Put *vbtop* back on **vbuff** in its original position.

8. Assign the value of *btop* to a new variable, *old-btop,* and get a new *btop*.

9. If *btop* is a conjunction or infix-function, then:

   a. Assign the value of *btop* to a new variable *btop2*.

   b. Try to instantiate *old-btop* as the second conjunct or operand of *btop*. If successful, then:

      i. Replace *btop*'s *pos:* slot-value by *case*. (*Btop* is now a conjunction with both conjuncts attached or an infix arithmetic function with both arguments attached. The value of *btop2* is not changed in this process.)

      ii. Try to initiate a relative clause construction with **tmp** and *btop*. (A new parse-state will be instantiated if this attempt is successful. Cleopatra's treatment of relative clauses is explained in the next chapter. This step also handles complex noun-phrases such as *the voltage at n1* as we shall see.)

iii. If the *x-v:* value of *btop* is *before-v*, then place *btop* and **tmp** on **buff** and instantiate a new parse-state. (*Btop* and **tmp** occur before the verb to which they will be attached. The integration procedure for that verb will retrieve these case-frames from **buff** and attach them to the verb-frame.) Else if the *x-v:* value is *after-v*, then try all "safe" attachments. (We explain what we mean by "safe" attachments in the next chapter. Many parse-states could be instantiated in this process.)

c. Place *btop2* on **buff**. (If *old-btop* is the head of a relative-clause, then it cannot be attached to *btop2* as yet.) Try to initiate a relative clause construction with **tmp** and *old-btop*.

d. Terminate the integration procedure.

10. (Control reaches here only if *btop* in step 9 is not a conjunction or infix-function.) Place *btop* back on **buff**, and assign the value of *old-btop* back to the variable *btop*. (This undoes step 8 above.)

11. If *btop* is a case, then try to initiate a relative clause construction with **tmp** and *btop*.

12. If *btop* is a clause-boundary-marker, then place *btop* and **tmp** on **buff**, and instantiate a new parse-state. Else if the *x-v:* value of *btop* is *before-v*, then place *btop* and **tmp** on **buff** and instantiate a new parse-state. Else if the *x-v:* value is *after-v*, then try all "safe" attachments. (The parenthetical remarks in step 9.b.iii apply here as well.)

13. Terminate the integration procedure.

4.3.2. The integration procedure for tense

The integration procedure for tense is called *tns*. When it is invoked, **tmp** contains the dictionary entry for the particular tense value (*present* or *past*). *Tns* is invoked with an argument, *carrier-v*, which is the name of the verb that is the tense carrier. If the tense carrier is an auxiliary element, then *carrier-v* is nil.

1. Get *btop*.

2. If *btop* is not a case or a clause boundary, then terminate the integration procedure. (This will discard parse-states in which verbal elements come immediately after determiners, adjectives, etc., and it will also discard incorrect noun-group hypotheses.)

3. Get the most recent element from **vbuff** and assign it to the variable *vbtop*.

4. If *vbtop* already contains tense information, then:

    a. Put *vbtop* back on **vbuff**, and *btop* back on **buff**.

    b. Instantiate a new parse-state. (Previous tense information over-rides **tmp**; the instantiated parse-state is substantially identical to the one the integration procedure started off in.)

    c. Terminate the integration procedure.

5. Get the tense value from the *value:* slot of **tmp** and add it to the *tns:* slot of *vbtop*.

6. If *carrier-v* is non-nil, then add *tns-on-verb* to the *features:* slot of *vbtop*.

7. If *btop* has *wh* on its *features:* slot (i.e. if *btop* is a noun phrase such as *what* or *what node*), and if *carrier-v* is *be* (i.e. the verb *to be*), then:

   a. If *btop* has *np* on its *type:* slot, then:

      i. Add *q* to the *mode:* slot of *vbtop*. (The clause is an interrogative one. However, there is an ambiguity associated with a sentence-initial *wh* when it is the only noun phrase before the verb *be*: The sentence *What is a dog?* could be answered by either *Rover is a dog* or by *A dog is a furry quadruped that barks* depending on whether the *wh* phrase was interpreted as the subject or the predicate. The next two steps handle the first interpretation; the following four the second.)

      ii. Put *btop* on **buff**.

      iii. Instantiate a new parse-state. (The *wh* phrase is expected to be the subject.)

      iv. Get *btop*. (This undoes step ii above.)

   b. Add *wh-fronted* to the *features:* slot of *btop* and to the *mode:* slot of *vbtop*.

   c. Put *btop* back on **buff**.

   d. Instantiate a new parse-state. (The *wh* phrase is expected to be the predicate.)

   e. Terminate the integration procedure.

8. If neither *prep-s* nor *relcl* is on the *type:* slot of *vbtop*, and *btop* is a clause-boundary-marker (i.e. the tense information

begins the sentence), then add *q*, *top-s*, and *y-n* on the *mode:* slot of *vbtop*. (The clause is the main clause of a yes-no question.)

9. Put *btop* on **buff**.

10. Put *vbtop* on **vbuff**.

11. Instantiate a new parse-state.

12. Terminate the integration procedure.

There is one detail that we have not covered in the algorithm above: There could be adverbs on **vbuff** that would be accessed before the clause-boundary-marker-frame that we have presumed to be the most recent element on **vbuff**. All these adverbs are removed from **vbuff** and stored in a list. Before *vbtop* is placed on **vbuff**, these adverbs are returned to **vbuff**.

While on the subject of adverbs, we should also reiterate that Cleopatra can only handle the adverbs *ever, never,* and *always*. A more complete adverbial vocabulary would require a far more sophisticated treatment of adverbs than is incorporated at present. One obvious source of difficulty is that adverbial clauses are placed on **buff** whereas adverbs are placed on **vbuff**, although both these constituents are functionally similar.

Chapter 5
Filling the Blanks

Now that the parsing mechanism has been elucidated, we can discuss some issues in detail. In this chapter, we describe the process of "safe" attachment to which we referred in the last chapter, we describe Cleopatra's treatment of relative clauses, adverbial clauses as objects of *after* and *before*, conjunctions, and ellipsis, and finally we return to the subject of confidence-levels.

First, however, we introduce the notation we use for depicting parse-states. We number parse-states with lower-case *s*'s, to distinguish them from sentences. Only three parse-state variables will concern us in this chapter: _*frames*_, _*buff*_, and _*vbuff*_. We enclose parse-states in braces, each of the variables in square brackets, and all frames in angle-brackets. For example, a final parse-state for the sentence:

What is the voltage at n1 at 5 ns?

is represented as:

```
s0.   {[*frames*  <be, <what>, <the-voltage>, <at-5-ns>>
                  <be, <^the-voltage>, <at-n1>>]
       [*buff*    nil]
       [*vbuff*   nil] }
```

For verb-frames , the first element within the angle-brackets is the name of the verb, and the other elements are case-fillers. (The case-roles of the fillers are not indicated.) The circumflex mark indicates that a case-frame is a (pronominal) reference to the case-frame with the name matching the symbol to the right of the circumflex. (Cleopatra treats *NP-PP* compounds as relative-clauses—more on this later.)

5.1. "Safe" Attachments

The attachment of a case-frame to a verb-frame is only attempted after it has been determined whether or not the case-frame is a relative-clause head or part of a conjunction or infix-function. This determination cannot be made until it has been determined, in turn, that no further words are left in the input or that a verbal element immediately follows the case-frame, or until another case-frame has been formed. (Handling extraposed relative clauses will necessitate some changes to Cleopatra.) When a case-frame is considered "safe" for attachment, its attachment to all "open" verb-frames can be attempted. We refer to these attachments as "safe" attachments. Safe attachments can have side-effects that include the attachment of other case-frames to verb-frames, and the "closings" of verb-frames. There are different varieties of safe attachments, and the side effects differ in each.

Let us first examine the safe attachment of a case-frame that is the last element on **buff** after all input words have been processed. Consider the sentence:

What is the voltage at n1 at 5 ns?

After the integration procedure for *ns* has been executed, one of the active parse-states will be:

s1. {[*frames* <be, <what>>
<be, <^the-voltage>, <at-n1>>]
[*buff* <S> <the-voltage> <S_r> <at-5-ns>]
[*vbuff* *nil*]}

In the above parse-state *<S>* is the clause-boundary-marker for the main clause, and *<S_r>* is the clause-boundary-marker for the relative clause.

After all the words in the sentence have been processed, the case-frames on **buff** are attached to verb-frames. Ambiguity is often manifested in this process. In our example, *<at-5-ns>* can be attached to either verb-frame. Let us follow both these possibilities:

1. *<At-5-ns>* is attached to the second verb-frame (the relative clause). The relative clause verb-frame is now *<be, <^the-voltage>, <at-n1>, <at-5-ns>>* and **buff** is now *<S> <the-voltage> <S_r>*.

   When the top (i.e. most recent) element on **buff** is a clause-marker (with an *x-v:* value of *after-v*, which is the case here), the "closing" of the corresponding verb-frame is attempted. (This attempt can fail if there are inconsistencies or contradictions in the *pending:* and *case-fills:* slots of the verb-frame, or if all the mandatory case-roles for the verb-frame have not been filled.) In this case, the attempt is successful. No further case-frames can now be attached to this verb-frame.

   The next element on **buff** is *<the-voltage>*. It is attached to the first verb-frame (the second is no longer "open" to further attachments). The *<S>* on **buff** causes this verb-frame to be closed too and finally a parse-state is instantiated that represents a completed parse:

s2. {[*frames* <be, <what>, <the-voltage>>
<be, <^the-voltage>, <at-n1>,
<at-5-ns>>]
[*buff* *nil*]
[*vbuff* *nil*]}

2. *<At-5-ns>* is not attached to the relative-clause verb-frame. Instead it is stored on an internal buffer. The next element on **buff** is *<S_r>*. This causes the relative-clause verb-frame to be closed (successfully). Frames on the internal buffer are effectively placed back on **buff**, which now reads: *[*buff* <S> <the-voltage> <at-5-ns>]*.

   The top element on **buff**, *<at-5-ns>*, is now attached to the main-verb-frame, as is the next element, *<the-voltage>*. After *<S>* triggers the closing of the main-verb-frame, another parse-state is instantiated that represents an alternative complete parse:

s3. {[*frames* <be, <what>, <the-voltage>,
<at-5-ns>>
<be, <^the-voltage>, <at-n1>>]
[*buff* *nil*]
[*vbuff* *nil*]}

Another safe attachment procedure is employed by integration procedures when **tmp** is a case-frame, and the top element on **buff** (let us call this *btop*) is also a case-frame. The difference between the above procedure (employed after all words have been processed) and this procedure (employed during the processing of a word) is that while in the former the goal is to attach all case-frames to verb-frames in all possible ways and to close all verb-frames, in the latter procedure the goal is to attach *btop* to all possible verb-frames, but, for each of these attachments, to only perform those other case-frame attachments and verb-frame closings which are necessary (for *btop*'s attachment to that particular verb-frame).

Let us take our example sentence again:

What is the voltage at n1 at 5 ns?

This time let us assume that the word *5* has just been read. At this point the parse-state is:

s4. {[*frames* <be, <what>> <be, <^the-voltage>>]
[*buff* <S> <the-voltage>
<S_r> <at-n1> <at>]}

The integration procedure for *5* is *generic-nouns-1*, which we described in the last chapter. In *generic-nouns-1*, *<at>* is attached to *<5>* (step 5). **Tmp** is now the case-frame *<at-5>*, and the top element on **buff** is also a case-frame (*<at-n1>*). All possible attachments of *<at-n1>* are tried.

The first possibility is that *<at-n1>* attaches to the relative-clause verb-frame. This attachment results in the following parse-state:

s5. {[*frames* <be, <what>>
<be, <^the-voltage>, <at-n1>>]
[*buff* <S> <the-voltage> <S_r> <at-5>]}

Note that this attachment did not require the relative-clause verb-frame to be closed, and it did not require *<the-voltage>* to be removed from **buff**. Note also that **tmp** is placed on **buff** before the parse-state is instantiated.

This is in fact the only parse-state that is instantiated here. The attachment of *<at-n1>* to the main-verb-frame requires that the relative-clause verb-frame first be closed. However, the attempted closing of this verb-frame will fail since its *pred* case-role (a nuclear case-role) has not been filled.

As we saw above, safe attachments are executed when both **tmp** and *btop* are case-frames, and when all input words have been processed. Another variation of safe attachments is employed when the integration procedure for a verb finds a case-frame on **buff** that has *after-v* on its *x-v:* slot. (In this case, the case-frame could be a case-filler of the previous verb-frame, or of the present one.) Some operations that the integration procedures for conjunctions and infix-functions perform also resemble safe attachments.

If a sentence is multiply ambiguous, and especially if each of many case-frames can be associated with more than one verb-frame, it is often the process of safe attachment that reveals the ambiguity. The number of new parse-states that could potentially be instantiated by a safe attachment is an exponential function of the number of "open" verb-frames in the original parse-state (for a given number of case-frames on **buff**). Of course, it is rarely the case that all potential parse-states really are instantiated; unsuccessful closings of verb-frames and unsuccessful attachments of case-frames to verb-frames usually restrict the number of new parse-states to a manageable few. We can think of the potential parse-states as syntactic possibilities, and of the unsuccessful closings and attachments as the application of semantic information to remove spurious ambiguity.

5.2. Relative Clauses

5.2.1. *That* Relative Clauses

Relative clauses signalled by the relative pronoun *that* can be handled straightforwardly (especially since Cleopatra does not handle *that*-complements). Let us consider a sentence with nested relative clauses:

S13. Is there a node that has a voltage that is greater than 5 volts at 5 ns?

Before the first *that* is read, the only active parse-state is:

s6. {[*frames* <be, <there>>]
[*buff* <S> <a-node>]
[*vbuff* *nil*]}

The integration procedure for *that* leads to the following parse-state:

s7. {[*frames* <be, <there>>]
[*buff* <S> <a-node> <S_r> <^a-node>]
[*vbuff* <S_r'>]}

<that> has been recognized as a reference to *<a-node>*. Both <S_r> and <S_r'> are clause boundary markers. <S_r'> will be removed by the integration procedure for the verb *have*. <S_r> will only be removed when the relative-clause verb is ultimately closed.

Before the second *that* is read, the only active parse-state is:

s8. {[*frames* <be, <there>> <has, <^a-node>>]
[*buff* <S> <a-node> <S_r> <a-voltage>]
[*vbuff* *nil*]}

And the integration procedure for *that* will result in the parse-state:

s9. {[*frames* <be, <there>> <has, <^a-node>>]
[*buff* <S> <a-node> <S_r> <a-voltage>
<S_{r2}> <^a-voltage>]
[*vbuff* <S_{r2}'>]}

5.2.2. *Whiz*-Deletion

It is a property of the English relative clause that when the relative pronoun is followed by a form of the verb *be*, both these words can be deleted. (The relative pronoun is often a *wh* pronoun, and *is* is the typical form of *be*, hence the name.)

Thus sentence *(S13)* can alternatively be stated as:

S14. Is there a node that has a voltage greater than 5 volts at 5 ns?

In this case, there is no explicit *that* to signal the second relative clause. Cleopatra instantiates a relative clause interpretation on the basis that *<a-voltage>* can be a subject and *<greater>* can be a predicate of the verb *be*. (Cleopatra actually instantiates two interpretations in this case. The other interpretation assumes that both *<a-voltage>* and *<greater>* are attached to the same verb, or to "sister" verbs.)

The active parse-state prior to reading *greater* in sentence *(S14)* is of course identical to state *(s8)*. The integration procedure for *greater*, however, will now lead to the parse-state:

s10. {[*frames* <be, <there>> <has, <^a-node>>
<be', <^a-voltage'>>]
[*buff* <S> <a-node> <S_r> <a-voltage>
<S_{r2}> <greater>]
[*vbuff* *nil*]}

Where the primes on the verb-frame *<be'>* and the case-frame *<^a-voltage'>* here indicate that Cleopatra distinguishes between these implicit frames and their explicit invocations (which would not have the primes).

Cleopatra analyzes *NP-PP* complex noun phrases as relative clauses under *whiz*-deletion too. For example, ***the voltage at n1*** is analyzed as if it were, in effect, ***the voltage that is at n1***. This generalization is not universally valid. *Of-PP*'s are especially problematic. ***The height of the building*** is grammatical, but ****The height that is of the building*** is not. *With-PP*'s can be accomodated as relative clauses with the additional stipulation that ***is with*** (in one sense of ***with***) becomes ***has*** (see [14;p.219]). Thus ***a node with a voltage*** becomes ***a node that has a voltage***.

The treatment of such complex noun phrases as relative clauses may not be justified theoretically, but it does permit the predication of attributes, properties, or arguments of nominals in straightforward manner. In any case, as we remarked above, Cleopatra does distinguish between *NP-PP* phrases and *NP-that-is-PP* phrases; the "implicit" relative-pronoun frame and relative-clause verb-frame are different (and can be arbitrarily so) from those invoked for the explicit relative-clause.

5.2.3. Relative pronoun deletion

The relative clause that is initiated in step 11 of ***generic-nouns-1*** (Section 4.3.1) is of the ***Whiz-deletion*** variety if ****tmp**** is a *pp*. If ****tmp**** is an ***np***, then another type of relative clause is possible. In this case, ****tmp**** is the subject of the relative clause, not the predicate, and the relative pronoun has been deleted.

Cleopatra can handle such relative clauses, although in its current domain there is little use for them. In a different but related domain, however, we could have sentences such as:

Show me the registers that the ALU contains?

which could just as naturally be expressed as:

Show me the registers the ALU contains?

5.2.4. Headless Relative Clauses

The type of relative clause that we call *headless* is exemplified by the sentence:

What is the voltage at n1 when the voltage at n2 reaches 2 volts?

(The relative clause here is the string *when the voltage at n2 reaches 2 volts.*) Such clauses are called *(Wh-Nominal) Relative Finite Clauses* by Winograd [77;p.476], and *Free Relatives* by Culicover [18;p.203].

A headless relative clause is instantiated when a noun-phrase immediately follows a *wh* noun-phrase or a *wh* prepositional-phrase. Cleopatra handles headless relative clauses by making the relative pronoun (*when*) a dummy head. If a tense morpheme is encountered before the case following *when*, the relative clause is disabled. This keeps main clauses from being parsed as relative clauses:

When does the voltage at n1 reach 2 volts?

On the other hand, when a *wh*-word and the next case are contiguous, the headless relative clause interpretation is not the only one instantiated. This allows ungrammatical but meaningful questions such as *When the voltage at n1 reaches 3 volts?* (It would be an easy matter to disable the main-clause interpretation in such cases and thereby reject such sentences.)

We conclude this section by showing the two parse-states, one for the relative-clause interpretation and one for the "linear" interpretation, resulting from the integration procedure for the first *voltage* in the sentence:

> When the voltage at n1 reaches 2 volts what is the voltage at n2?

s11. {[*frames* *nil*]
[*buff* <S> <when>
<S_r> <^when> <the-voltage>]
[*vbuff* <S'> <S_r'>]}

s12. {[*frames* *nil*]
[*buff* <S> <when> <the-voltage>]
[*vbuff* <S'>]}

5.3. Time-Adverbial Clauses

The only remaining class of subordinate clause that Cleopatra can handle currently is the adverbial clause as object of the preposition *after* or *before*:

S15. What is the voltage at n1 after the voltage at n2 reaches 3 volts?

Since *after* and *before* can also take nominal objects (as in *after 5 ns*, for example), Cleopatra treats these prepositions as ambiguous. Thus there are separate dictionary and integration procedures for the sentential-object and nominal-object senses of *after* and *before*. Assume that the parse-state before *after* is read in sentence *(S15)* is:

s13. {[*frames* <be, <what>, <the-voltage>>]
[*buff* <S> <at-n1>]
[*vbuff* *nil*]}

The integration procedures for the two senses of *after* would then each instantiate one new parse-state:

s14. {[*frames* <be, <what>, <the-voltage>>]
[*buff* <S> <at-n1> <after> <S$_a$>]
[*vbuff* *nil*]}

s15. {[*frames* <be, <what>, <the-voltage>>]
[*buff* <S> <at-n1> <after$_2$>]
[*vbuff* <S$_a$'>]}

(State *(s13)* is the simpler of the two parse-states that would be active at that point. In the other, *<at-n1>* is treated as the predicate of a relative-clause, as described in Section 5.2.2.)

Eventually state *(s14)* will lead to the final parse-state:

s16. {[*frames* <be, <what>, <the-voltage$_1$>,
<after-S$_a$>>
<be, <^the-voltage$_1$>, <at-n1>>
<be, <^the-voltage$_2$>, <at-n2>>
<reach, <the-voltage$_2$>, <3-volts>>]
[*buff* *nil*]
[*vbuff* *nil*]}

We refer to case-frames such as *<after-S$_a$>* as *prep-S* case-frames in general. *Prep-S* case-frames have a *verb:* slot that indicates what the verb of the adverbial clause is. In our example, the *verb:* slot for *<after-S$_a$>* will be filled by (the surrogate id for) the verb-frame *<reach>*.

Though sentences such as *(S15)* are used to specify time-intervals, similar constructions can be used to specify time-points:

What is the voltage at n1 5 ns after the voltage at n2 reaches 3 volts?

What is the voltage at n1 at 5 ns after the voltage at n2 reaches 3 volts?

Cleopatra can handle such sentences (in which the adverbial clause takes a time-value prefix) as well.

5.4. Conjunctions

Conjunction, as a linguistic device, promotes economy of expression; intentions that would take multiple queries to express without using conjunctions can be expressed in one query. Thus a circuit-designer could use the sentence:

S16. What are the voltages at n1 and n2 at 5 and 10 ns?

instead of the longer and more laborious sequence:

S17. What is the voltage at n1 at 5 ns?

What is the voltage at n1 at 10 ns?

What is the voltage at n2 at 5 ns?

S18. What is the voltage at n2 at 10 ns?

More significantly for our purposes, conjunction increases expressive power. Sentences such as the following do not have conjunction-free synonymous renderings (unless yet other constructions are introduced):

S19. What is the sum of the voltages at n1 and n2?

S20. What is the maximum voltage at n1 between 5 and 10 ns?

Cleopatra can interpret simple nominal conjunctions—the conjuncts must each be single case-frames. Thus the following sentences (as well as sentences *(S16)*, *(S19)*, and *(S20)*) are accepted:

What is the voltage at n1 and n2?

What is the voltage at n1 and at n2?

What is the voltage at n1 and the voltage at n2 at 10 ns?

S21. What is the sum of the voltage at n1 and the voltage at n2 at 5 ns?

What is the voltage at n1 after 5 ns and before the voltage at n2 reaches 5 volts?

What is the voltage at n1 after the voltage at n2 reaches 5 volts and before the voltage at n3 reaches 3 volts?

S22. What is the voltage at n1 and n2 and n3 at 5 and 10 ns?

Sentence *(S21)* is interpreted as synonymous with *At 5 ns, what is the sum of the voltage at n1 and the voltage at n2?* Note that more than two conjuncts can be used as in sentence *(S22)*.

Sentences such as the following fall outside of Cleopatra's coverage at present:

S23. What is the voltage at n1 and what is the voltage at n2?

S24. What is the voltage at n1 at 5 ns and at n2 at 10 ns?

In sentence *(S23)*, the conjuncts are not case-frames, but entire sentences. In sentence *(S24)*, the conjuncts are multiple case-frames.

Cleopatra handles conjunctions by instantiating in parallel, when the word *and* is read, parse-states that represent all possible choices for the first conjunct. All but one of these choices will not be the most recent case-frame on **buff**, and in these cases some case-frame-to-verb-frame attachments and some verb-frame closings will be performed before the parse-state is instantiated. (This process is similar to a safe attachment.)

An example might illuminate the procedure. Consider the sentence:

S25. What is the voltage at n1 and . . .?

The relevant parse-state when *and* is read is:

s17. {[*frames* <be, <what>> <be, <^the-voltage>>]
[*buff* <S> <the-voltage> <S_r> <at-n1>]
[*vbuff* *nil*]}

The integration procedure for *and* will instantiate two new parse-states:

s18. {[*frames* <be, <what>> <be, <^the-voltage>>]
[*buff* <S> <the-voltage>
<S_r> <and, <at-n1>>]
[*vbuff* *nil*]}

s19. {[*frames* <be, <what>>
<be, <^the-voltage>, <at-n1>>]
[*buff* <S> <and, <the-voltage>>]
[*vbuff* *nil*]}

Note that the relative-clause verb-frame in state *(s19)* (but not in *(s18)*) has been closed.

Depending on how sentence *(S25)* is continued, either state *(s18)* or *(s19)* will lead to the correct interpretation. If the ellipsis in *(S25)* is replaced by ***n2***, then the final parse-state will be:

```
s20.  {[*frames*  <be, <what>, <the-voltage>>
                  <be, <^the-voltage>,
                          <and , <at-n1>, <n2>>>]
       [*buff*    nil]
       [*vbuff*   nil]}
```

If *at n2* is used instead of ***n2***, then the resulting parse-state would be identical to the above except that <***n2***> would be replaced by <*at-n2*> in the conjunction-frame. If, on the other hand, the ellipsis is replaced by *the voltage at n2*, the final parse-state will be:

```
s21.  {[*frames*  <be, <what>,
                          <and,
                              <the-voltage_1>,<the-voltage_2>>>
                  <be, <^the-voltage_1>, <at-n1>>
                  <be, <^the-voltage_2>, <at-n2>>]
       [*buff*    nil]
       [*vbuff*   nil]}
```

One issue we have not discussed here is the basis on which a pair of case-frames are judged to be valid conjuncts for a conjunction. Thus state *(s18)* is terminated (more precisely, its lineage is) if the ellipsis replacement is *the voltage at n2* because *<and, <at-n1>, <the-voltage>>* is rejected as a valid conjunction. The rules for what constitutes a valid conjunction and what does not will be enumerated later in this chapter.

Incidentally, infix arithmetic functions (*plus*, *minus*, *times*) are processed similarly to conjunctions. The additional constraint on arithmetic functions—that both operands must be "quantities"—results in relatively fewer parse-states being instantiated.

5.5. Ellipses

Like conjunctions, ellipses aid economy of expression. In this case, though, the economy is manifested not by the reduced number of queries, but in their brevity. To use an example from the previous section again, the designer could express sentences *(S17)-(S18)* as:

What is the voltage at n1 at 5 ns?

At n2?

At 10 ns?

At n1?

Cleopatra can handle such forms of ellipses. In fact, Cleopatra allows the substitution of multiple case-frames as well:

S26. When is the voltage at n1 greater than 3 volts?

S27. The voltage at n2 less than 2 volts?

S28. At n3 than 4?

A sentence fragment is recognized as elliptic when all the verb-frames on **frames** (if any) have been successfully closed, but case-frames still remain on **buff**. If any verb-frames do exist on **frames**, they must all represent subordinate-clause verbs which have either their head case-frames (in the case of relative clauses), or their *prep-S* case-frames (in the case of adverbial clauses), on **buff**.

Consider sentences *(S26)* and *(S27)* again. The final parse-state for sentence *(S26)* is:

```
s22.  {[*frames*  <be, <when>, <the-voltage>,
                       <greater>, <than-3-v>>
                  <be, <^the-voltage>, <at-n1>>]
       [*buff*    nil]
       [*vbuff*   nil]}
```

Sentence *(S27)* results in the parse-state:

```
s23.  {[*frames*  <be, <^the-voltage>, <at-n2>>]
       [*buff*    <S> <the-voltage> <less>
                      <than-2-volts>]
       [*vbuff*   nil]}
```

In order to resolve the ellipsis, Cleopatra has to identify the case-frame in state *(s22)* (the *referent* case-frame) that each case-frame on **buff** in state *(s23)* is intended to replace. The referent can be ambiguous: A query such as *When is the voltage at n1 greater than the voltage at n2?* could be followed by *the voltage at n3?* Furthermore, a particular choice of substitution could remove some case-frames as possible referents: If the referent case-frame is a *prep-S* case-frame or a relative-clause-head case-frame, then all the case-frames attached to the *prep-S* verb-frame, or the relative-clause verb-frame, cannot be potential referents for other substitutions.

Ellipsis substitution, then, is not always straightforward, and Cleopatra employs a somewhat brute-force approach. Each case-frame on **buff** is matched against each case-frame in the final parse-state for the previous sentence. This matching process is similar to a confidence-level updating process and is described in detail in the next section. If the match indicates any degree of acceptability (i.e. returns a non-zero number), then the verb-frames (if any) in the previous parse-state whose case-frames would not remain possible referents if the substitution was actually done, are also computed. Both the number returned by the matching process, and this list of verb-frames, are stored as separate fields of one entry in an array. The array is best thought of as two-dimensional, with as many rows as there are case-frames on **buff**, and as many columns as there are case-frames attached to the verb-frames in the parse-state of the previous sentence.

The problem of generating an acceptable set of substitutions is then equivalent to selecting an entry from each row of the array such that the numeric part of the entry is non-zero, and such that there is no selection from any column that represents a case-frame attached to a verb-frame that is listed on the verb-frames field of any selected entry. At present, Cleopatra assumes that an entry from each row can be selected such that the numeric part of that entry is not lower than the numeric part of any of the other entries in that row. If this assumption is satisfied, Cleopatra will generate an optimal set of substitutions; if not, the ellipsis will not be resolved. On the basis of our experience with Cleopatra, the assumption seems justified.

After the set of referent case-frames has been determined, some further processing may still be needed. If both the referent case-frame and the new case-frame represent cardinal numbers, but only the referent case-frame has a *units:* slot-value, a *units:* slot with the same value is appended to the new case-frame. More involuted processing is needed if the referent case-frame is a relative-clause head, but the new case-frame is not. (For example, if *What is the sum of the voltages at n1 and n2?* was followed by *The difference?*) In such cases, Cleopatra adds a new relative-clause verb-frame to **frames**. This verb-frame is identical to the relative-clause verb-frame (from the previous query) that has the referent case-frame as its head, except that the head is now the new case-frame. Other case-fillers of this verb-frame may be relative-clause heads or *prep-S* case-frames, and their relative-clause or *prep-S* verb-frames will also be added to **frames** (this operation being done recursively).

The ellipsis resolution will eventually instantiate a final parse-state for sentence *(S27)*:

s24. {[*frames* <be, <when>, <the-voltage>, <less>,
<than-2-v>>
<be, <^the-voltage>, <at-n2>>]
[*buff* *nil*]
[*vbuff* *nil*]}

And sentence *(S28)* will eventually lead to:

s25. {[*frames* <be, <when>, <the-voltage>, <less>,
<than-4-v>>
<be, <^the-voltage>, <at-n3>>]
[*buff* *nil*]
[*vbuff* *nil*]}

The ellipses we have discussed above have all been ***inter-sentential*** ellipses. There are also ***intra-sentential*** ellipses, in which the referent case-frame is in the same sentence and not the previous one. Thus instead of the query ***What is the voltage at n1 after the voltage at n2 reaches 3 volts?*** the designer could use an intra-sentential ellipsis:

S29. What is the voltage at n1 after n2 reaches 3 volts?

An ability to handle sentences such as *(S29)* would undeniably be useful. Cleopatra does not provide such an ability at present, but later on we outline how intra-sentential ellipses might be treated within Cleopatra's framework (see p. 133).

5.6. Confidence-Levels Revisited

In our otherwise fairly detailed discussion of the last two chapters, we have assumed that every interpretation is a yes-or-no proposition, and that parallel parse-states are equivalent. These assumptions, although false, have enabled our discussion to be much more focussed than it would otherwise have been. It is the notion of confidence-levels (see Section 3.2.2) that allows Cleopatra to differentiate between likely and unlikely-but-possible parse-states, and in this section we elaborate on how confidence-levels work within the parsing process.

Initially, the confidence level is set to *10*. During the parse, whenever a construction is encountered that is short of ideal in any way, the confidence-level can be decremented. Syntactic deviations, such as not having an article before a count-noun, or even minor ones such as substituting a noun-phrase for a prepositional phrase in an elliptic expression, as well as semantic discrepancies between conjuncts or in elliptic constructions, can all lead to varying reductions in the confidence-level. Mostly, however, confidence-level changes are wrought in case-frame-to-verb-frame attachments, conjunctions, and ellipsis-processing.

5.6.1. Attaching case-frames to verb-frames

When an attachment of a case-frame to a verb-frame is attempted, a set of possible case-roles that the case-frame can fill is generated. (If the set is singular, the case-frame will be placed on the *case-fills:* slot, otherwise it will be placed on the *pending:* slot.) If there is a nuclear case-role in this set (recall that a nuclear case-role is one that is listed on the *cases:* slot of the verb-frame), or if the case-frame is a relative-pronoun, or if the case-frame is a *wh*-fronted phrase, then the confidence-level will not be altered. If there is no nuclear case-role in the set of possible case-roles, but all the nuclear case-roles that have not been filled have candidate fillers already on the *pendings:* slot, then the confidence-level is decremented by *2*. Otherwise the confidence-level is decremented by *4*. (There are some minor differences between the attachments of pre-verbal and post-verbal cases which need not concern us.)

Thus there is a bias against extranuclear cases. If a case-frame fills a nuclear case-role in one parse-state and an extranuclear one in another, the former parse-state will recieve a higher rating. For example, the sentence *What is the voltage at n1?* leads to two final parse-states. In the first parse-state, *<at-n1>* is attached as an extranuclear case-filler of the main verb, and in the second *<at-n1>* is attached as a nuclear case-filler of a relative-clause verb. The latter interpretation will be favored although it postulates an additional verb-frame. (Relative-clause instantiations trigger confidence-level decrements too, but not when the relative clause has a "function-noun" for its subject, and an "argument-noun" for its predicate.)

5.6.2. Concordance of conjuncts

As we said before, Cleopatra handles conjunctions by instantiating a separate parse-state for each possible first conjunct. As further case-frames are formed, they will be considered as possible second conjuncts for each of the half-filled conjunctions. The greater the concordance (both syntactic and semantic) between the first and (prospective) second conjunct, the greater the confidence-level of the corresponding parse-state. We detail precisely how the degree of concordance is calculated, and how it affects the confidence-level:

1. Set the variable x to *0*.

2. If both conjuncts have *function-noun* on their *features:* slots, then add *5* to x.

   Else if one conjunct has *t-value* (for *time-value*) on its *features:* slot, but the other does not, then return failure. (Conjunction not possible.)

   Else if both conjuncts have *t-value* on their *features:* slots, then:

   a. If either conjunct has *wh* on its *features:* slot but does not have *relcl-head* on its *features:* slot, then return failure. (*When* can only be a conjunct if it is the relative-pronoun of a headless relative clause.)

   b. If both conjuncts have *t-point* (for *time-point*) on their *features:* slots, or if both have *t-interval* on their *features:* slots, then add *5* to x.

   c. Else add *3* to x. (One conjunct is a time-point, the other a time-interval.)

   Else if both conjuncts have *cardinal* on their *features:* slots, then add *5* to x.

   Else if both conjuncts have *node-id* on their *features:* slots, then add *5* to x.

   Else if both conjuncts have *quantity* on their *features:* slots, then add *3* to x.

   Else return failure.

3. If both conjuncts have *relcl-head* on their *features:* slots, then add *2* to x.

   Else if neither conjunct has *relcl-head* on its *features:* slot, then add *2* to x.

4. If both conjuncts have *pp* on their *type:* slots, then:

   a. If both conjuncts have *prep-s* (prepositions with sentential objects) on their *type:* slots, then add *3* to x.

      Else if neither conjunct has *prep-s* on its *type:* slot, then add *3* to x.

      Else add *1* to x. (One conjunct is a preposition with a sentential object; the other is a preposition with a nominal object.)

   Else if both conjuncts have *np* on their *type:* slots, then add *3* to x.

   Else if the first conjunct has both *pp* and *2-objects* on its *type:* slot, then add *3* to x. (This keeps phrases such as *between 5 and 10 ns* and *sum of 1 and 2* from being penalized—the conjuncts here are a prepositional-phrase and a noun-phrase.)

   Else if the first conjunct has *pp* on its *type:* slot, and the second conjunct has *np* on its *type:* slot, then add *1* to x. (*PP*-and-*NP* conjunctions are better than *NP*-and-*PP* conjunctions.)

5. The confidence-level for the parse-state corresponding to the conjunction is reduced by *10* - x, or not at all if x is greater than 10.

All these numbers are, of course, ad-hoc. Significant extensions of domain might require some changes, both in the numbers and in the steps of the procedure. (The validity of a conjunction is, in any case, highly domain-dependent.) One feasible extension that would make the conjunction evaluation procedure largely domain-independent would be to incorporate a *category:* slot for case-frames, and a hierarchical network of all possible values for the *category:* slots. Then, instead of testing for particular features, we could use the network to determine how "close" semantically the *category:* slot-values of the two conjuncts are; the closer they are, the higher the confidence-level-factor for the conjunction. (There is independent justification for a hierarchical network of semantic categories—see pp. 25-26.)

5.6.3. Substitutions in Ellipses

We now describe how the acceptability measure of a case-frame as a substitute for another case-frame in an elliptic query is calculated. The acceptability measure does not directly affect the confidence-level of a parse-state. Ultimately, however, when the set of referent case-frames (see Section 5.5) is determined, the acceptability measures of these case-frames (for their particular substitutes) will affect the confidence-level of the final parse-state.

In the following algorithm, *old-c* is a case-frame from the previous query which is being tested as a referent for *new-c*, a case-frame left on **buff** after the regular processing of the current query has been completed. *Cas-rol* is the case-role that *old-c* filled. A returned value of zero implies that *new-c* cannot substitute for *old-c*.

1. If *cas-rol* is not one of the case-roles indicated on the *cases-for:* slot of *new-c*, then return *0*. (*New-c* cannot fill the case-role that *old-c* filled.)

2. If *old-c* has *relpro* on its *type:* slot, then return *0*. (A relative pronoun is not a candidate for substitution.)

3. Assign the value *0* to the variable x.

4. If both ***new-c*** and ***old-c*** have ***t-point*** on their ***features:*** slots, then add *3* to x.

   Else if both ***new-c*** and ***old-c*** have ***t-interval*** on their ***features:*** slots, then add *3* to x.

   Else if both ***new-c*** and ***old-c*** have ***t-value*** on their ***features:*** slots, then add *2* to x. (One of ***new-c*** and ***old-c*** is a ***t-point***, the other a ***t-interval***.)

   Else if both have ***function-noun*** on their ***features:*** slots, then add *2* to x.

   Else if both have ***arg-n*** (for ***argument-noun***) on their ***features:*** slots, then add *2* to x.

   Else if both have ***comparative*** on their ***type:*** slots, then add *4* to x. (Substituting ***less*** for ***greater***, for example.)

   Else if both have ***adj-pred*** on their ***type:*** slots, then add *3* to x. (***Maximum*** for ***minimum***, for example.)

   Else if both have ***number*** on their ***type:*** slots, then add *3* to x.

   Else if both have ***arith-function*** on their ***features:*** slots, then add *4* to x.

5. If the ***value:*** slot-value of ***old-c*** is the same as the ***value:*** slot-value of ***new-c***, then add *2* to x. (Having the same ***value:*** is really only a positive factor if both case-frames are relative-clause heads. Perhaps if this is not the case, some amount should even be deducted from x.)

6. If x is *0*, then return *0*. (All the above tests were semantic. If there is no semantic similarity between *old-c* and *new-c*, syntactic similarities are not even considered.)

7. If both *old-c* and *new-c* have *np* on their *type:* slots, then add *1* to x.

   Else if both have *pp* on their *type:* slots, then add *2* to x.

8. If both *new-c* and *old-c* have *relcl-head* on their *features:* slots, then:

   a. Add *1* to x.

   b. Get the associated relative-clause verbs for both *new-c* and *old-c*.

   c. If the *name:* slot-values for both verbs are identical, then:

      i. Add *2* to x.

      ii. If both verbs have the same number of filled case-roles, then add *1* to x.

9. Return x.

The extension that we indicated at the end of the last subsection would help here too. A *category:* slot could be used analogously to its projected use with the conjunction construction (p. 88) in order to make confidence-level updates for ellipses less domain-dependent.

Chapter 6
Some Detailed Examples

In this chapter we analyze in detail the parsing of three sentences. We will go through each sentence word-by-word (and, where necessary, morpheme-by-morpheme) showing most of the parse-states instantiated. In order to include confidence-levels in these analyses, we extend our notation for parse-states by including a bracketing for **sconf** (the parse-state variable that indicates the confidence-level of the parse-state).

The initial parse-state for all sentences is:

s0. {[*frames* *nil*]
[*buff* <S>]
[*vbuff* <S'>]
[*sconf* 10]}

We will number the parse-states in each example from *s1*.

6.1. Example 1

The first sentence we consider is relatively straightforward, except for the conjoined node-identifiers:

S30. What are the voltages at n1 and n2 at 5 ns?

What: Cleopatra knows about two senses for the word *what*: the interrogative-pronoun sense (*<what>*), and the determiner sense (*<what$_d$>*). Hence two parse-states are instantiated:

(s0) →

```
s1.   {[*frames*  nil]
       [*buff*    <S> <what>]
       [*vbuff*   <S'>]
       [*sconf*   10]}

s2.   {[*frames*  nil]
       [*buff*    <S> <what_d>]
       [*vbuff*   <S'>]
       [*sconf*   10]}
```

Are: First, the present tense morpheme is processed. The integration procedure for tense recognizes state *(s2)* to be incorrect (a determiner must be followed by a noun). State *(s1)* leads to two new states in which a *tns:* slot-value is added to *<S'>* to indicate present tense. In one of these states *<what>* is assumed to be fronted (i.e. it is assumed that *<what>* does not fill the *subj* case-role), while in the other *<what>* is assumed to be non-fronted (i.e. *<what>* must fill the *subj* case-role). We indicate the non-fronted *<what>* as *<what$_{nf}$>*.

(s1) →

```
s3.   {[*frames*  nil]
       [*buff*    <S> <what_nf>]
       [*vbuff*   <S'>]
       [*sconf*   10]}

s4.   {[*frames*  nil]
       [*buff*    <S> <what>]
       [*vbuff*   <S'>]
       [*sconf*   10]}
```

The integration procedure for the root-verb morpheme will attempt to attach <*what*> (or <*what*$_{nf}$>) to the verb-frame <*be*>. However, the dictionary entry for *what* does not list the *subj* case-role in its *cases-for:* slot. Thus the parse-state with the non-fronted <*what*$_{nf}$> will be terminated, while in the other parse-state <*what*> will be attached to the verb-frame. (Specifically, <*what*> will be placed on the verb-frame's *pending:* slot.)

(s4) ⟶

```
s5.   {[*frames*  <be, <what>>]
       [*buff*    <S>]
       [*vbuff*   nil]
       [*sconf*   10]}
```

The: The definite article has one sense, with one morpheme, and the integration procedure for that morpheme places the determiner-frame <*the*> on **buff**.

(s5) ⟶

```
s6.   {[*frames*  <be, <what>>]
       [*buff*    <S> <the>]
       [*vbuff*   nil]
       [*sconf*   10]}
```

Voltages: *Voltages* has two morphemes, the root noun *voltage* and the plural suffix *-s*. Cleopatra ignores the latter. The integration procedure for *voltage* will attach <*the*> to the noun-frame <*voltage*> to form the case-frame <*the-voltage*>, which is then placed on **buff**.

(s6) ⟶

s7. {[*frames* <be, <what>>]
[*buff* <S> <the-voltage>]
[*vbuff* *nil*]
[*sconf* 10]}

At: The integration procedure for *at* checks to see if there is a case-frame on the *pending:* slot of an open verb-frame such that the possible case-roles list of that case-frame includes an asterisk. The case-frame *<what>* satisfies this condition. An attachment of *<at>* to *<what>* is attempted. This attempt fails since the *marker-for:* slot of *<at>* and the *cases-for:* slot of *<what>* have no case-role in common. Only the following parse-state is instantiated:

(s7) →

s8. {[*frames* <be, <what>>]
[*buff* <S> <the-voltage> <at>]
[*vbuff* *nil*]
[*sconf* 10]}

N1: The preposition-frame *<at>* is attached to the noun-frame *<n1>* to form the case-frame *<at-n1>*. Two new parse-states are instantiated, one each for the relative-clause and the "linear" interpretation (see Section 5.2.2). The high confidence-level of the relative-clause interpretation causes a reduction in the confidence-level of the linear interpretation.

(s8) →

s9. {[*frames* <be, <what>> <be, <^the-voltage>>]
[*buff* <S> <the-voltage> <S_r> <at-n1>]
[*vbuff* *nil*]
[*sconf* 10]}

```
s10.  {[*frames*  <be, <what>, <the-voltage>>]
       [*buff*    <S> <at-n1>]
       [*vbuff*   nil]
       [*sconf*   6]}
```

And: State *(s9)* allows both *<at-n1>* and *<the-voltage>* to be possible first conjuncts, whereas state *(s10)* allows just *<at-n1>*.

(s9) ⟶

```
s11.  {[*frames*  <be, <what>> <be, <^the-voltage>>]
       [*buff*    <S> <the-voltage>
                  <S_r> <and,<at-n1>>]
       [*vbuff*   nil]
       [*sconf*   10]}

s12.  {[*frames*  <be, <what>>
                  <be, <^the-voltage>, <at-n1>>]
       [*buff*    <S> <and,<the-voltage>>]
       [*vbuff*   nil]
       [*sconf*   10]}
```

(s10) ⟶

```
s13.  {[*frames*  <be, <what>, <the-voltage>>]
       [*buff*    <S> <and, <at-n1>>]
       [*vbuff*   nil]
       [*sconf*   6]}
```

In state *(s12)*, the second verb-frame has been closed.

N2: In all the three active states, the top element on **buff** is an incomplete conjunction, and this causes *<n2>* to be placed on **buff**.

(s11) ⟶

s14. {[*frames* <be, <what>> <be, <^the-voltage>>]
[*buff* <S> <the-voltage>
<S_r> <and, <at-n1>> <n2>]
[*vbuff* *nil*]
[*sconf* 10]}

(s12) ⟶

s15. {[*frames* <be, <what>>
<be, <^the-voltage>, <at-n1>>]
[*buff* <S> <and, <the-voltage>> <n2>]
[*vbuff* *nil*]
[*sconf* 10]}

(s13) ⟶

s16. {[*frames* <be, <what>, <the-voltage>>]
[*buff* <S> <and, <at-n1>> <n2>]
[*vbuff* *nil*]
[*sconf* 6]}

At: *<At>* is also placed on **buff**.

(s14) ⟶

s17. {[*frames* <be, <what>> <be, <^the-voltage>>]
[*buff* <S> <the-voltage>
<S_r> <and,<at-n1>> <n2> <at>]
[*vbuff* *nil*]
[*sconf* 10]}

(s15) ⟶

s18. {[*frames* <be, <what>>
<be, <^the-voltage>, <at-n1>>]
[*buff* <S> <and,<the-voltage>> <n2> <at>]
[*vbuff* *nil*]
[*sconf* 10]}

(s16) ⟶

s19. {[*frames* <be, <what>, <the-voltage>>]
[*buff* <S> <and,<at-n1>> <n2> <at>]
[*vbuff* *nil*]
[*sconf* 6]}

5: The preposition-frame *<at>* and the noun-frame *<5>* form the case-frame *<at-5>*. In each of the active parse-states, the two most recent elements on **buff** (prior to *<at>*) are a case-frame (*<n2>* in each state) and an incomplete conjunction-frame. *<N2>* is tried as the second conjunct. If successful, the conjunction is attached to a verb-frame. States *(s17)* and *(s19)* lead to one new parse-state each; state *(s18)* is terminated. The conjunct match between *<at-n1>* and *<n2>* reduces the confidence-levels by *2*.

(s17) ⟶

s20. {[*frames* <be, <what>>
<be, <^the-voltage>,
<and, <at-n1>, <n2>>]
[*buff* <S> <the-voltage> <S_r> <at-5>]
[*vbuff* *nil*]
[*sconf* 8]}

(s19) ⟶

```
s21.  {[*frames*  <be, <what>, <the-voltage>,
                       <and, <at-n1>, <n2>>]
       [*buff*    <S> <at-5>]
       [*vbuff*   nil]
       [*sconf*   4]}
```

Ns: A *units:* slot is added to each of the case-frames *<at-5>* with the value *ns*.

(s20) ⟶

```
s22.  {[*frames*  <be, <what>>
                  <be, <^the-voltage>,
                       <and, <at-n1>, <n2>>]
       [*buff*    <S> <the-voltage> <S_r> <at-5-ns>]
       [*vbuff*   nil]
       [*sconf*   8]}
```

(s21) ⟶

```
s23.  {[*frames*  <be, <what>, <the-voltage>,
                       <and, <at-n1>, <n2>>]
       [*buff*    <S> <at-5-ns>]
       [*vbuff*   nil]
       [*sconf*   4]}
```

?: (Although input to Cleopatra cannot contain punctuation, we use the question-mark here as an indicator that there are no further words left in the input.) Recognition that all the words have been processed triggers the attempted attachments of all case-frames on **buff** and closings of all verb-frames on **frames**.

(s22) ⟶

```
s24.  {[*frames*  <be,<what>,<the-voltage>,<at-5-ns>>
                  <be, <^the-voltage>,
                       <and, <at-n1>, <n2>>]
       [*buff*    nil]
       [*vbuff*   nil]
       [*sconf*   7]}

s25.  {[*frames*  <be, <what>, <the-voltage>>
                  <be, <^the-voltage>,
                       <and, <at-n1>, <n2>>,
                       <at-5-ns>>]
       [*buff*    nil]
       [*vbuff*   nil]
       [*sconf*   4]}
```

(s23) ⟶

```
s26.  {[*frames*  <be, <what>, <the-voltage>,
                       <and,<at-n1>,<n2>>,<at-5-ns>>]
       [*buff*    nil]
       [*vbuff*   nil]
       [*sconf*   4]}
```

Thus we are left with three valid parse-states. The confidence-levels shown above reflect a final confidence-level evaluation process that benefits parse-states with most attachments to the main-verb (though not by enough to change the best-rated interpretation in this case).

The figure on the next page depicts the tree-structure produced by the parsing process for sentence *(S30)*. (We do not show the parse-state trees for the other examples, since the degrees of branching in their parses are relatively small.)

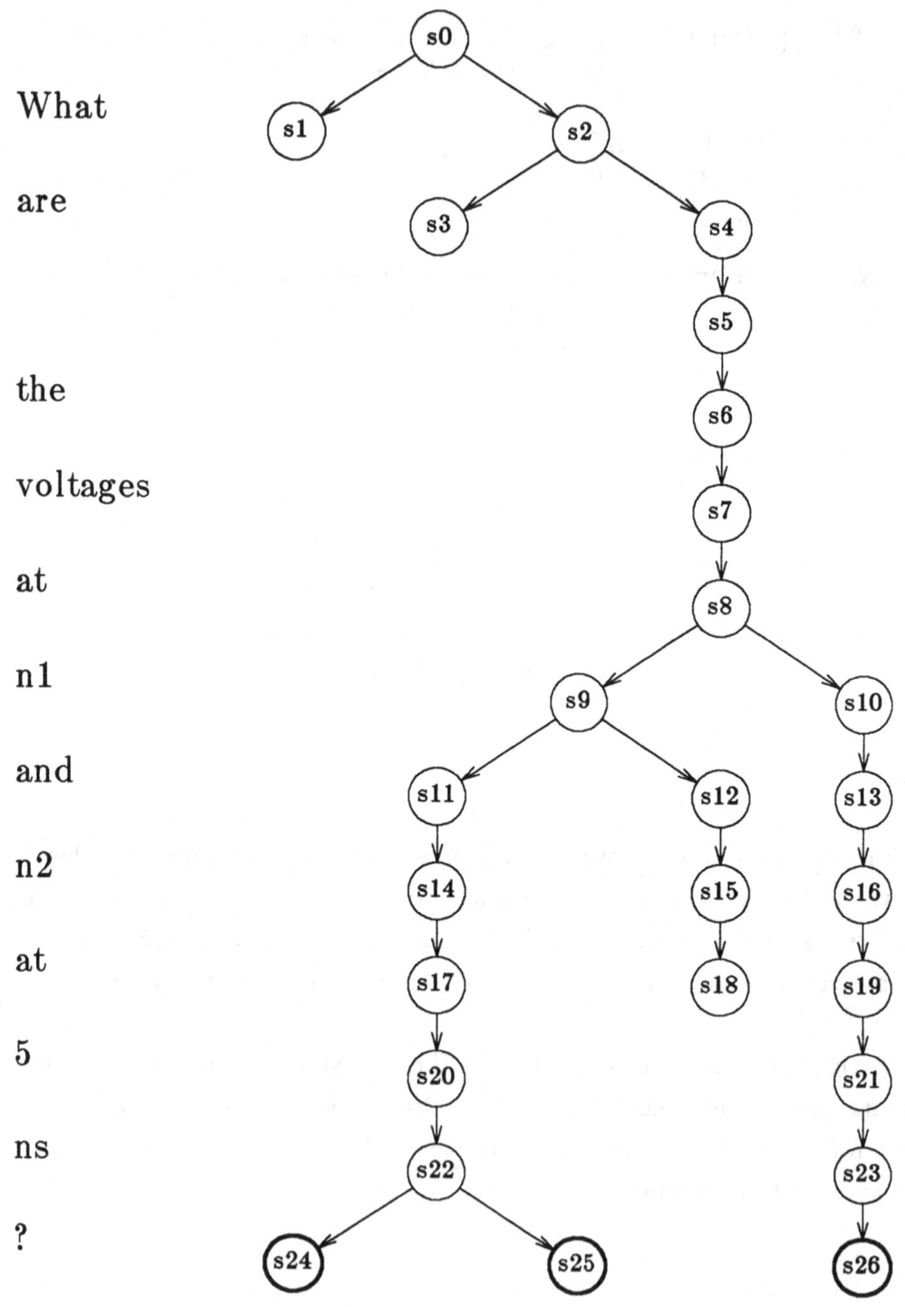
What
are
the
voltages
at
n1
and
n2
at
5
ns
?
s0
s1
s2
s3
s4
s5
s6
s7
s8
s9
s10
s11
s12
s13
s14
s15
s16
s17
s18
s19
s20
s21
s22
s23
s24
s25
s26

6.2. Example 2

Our second sentence has a fronted prepositional phrase, and a fronted *wh* noun phrase which is the object of a trailing preposition:

S31. At 5 ns which node is the voltage maximum at?

The initial parse-state is again *(s0)* (p. 93).

At: The preposition-frame *<at>* is placed on **buff**.

(s0) →

```
s1.   {[*frames*  nil]
       [*buff*    <S> <at>]
       [*vbuff*   nil]
       [*sconf*   10]}
```

5: *<At>* is attached to *<5>* to form the case-frame *<at-5>*, which is then placed on **buff**.

(s1) →

```
s2.   {[*frames*  nil]
       [*buff*    <S> <at-5>]
       [*vbuff*   nil]
       [*sconf*   10]}
```

Ns: A *units:* slot is added to the case-frame *<at-5>* with the value *ns*.

(s2) →

s3. {[*frames* *nil*]
[*buff* <S> <at-5-ns>]
[*vbuff* *nil*]
[*sconf* 10]}

Which: Cleopatra recognizes only the determiner sense of *which*. The determiner-frame *<which>* is placed on *buff*.

(s3) ⟶

s4. {[*frames* *nil*]
[*buff* <S> <at-5-ns> <which>]
[*vbuff* *nil*]
[*sconf* 10]}

Node: *<Which>* is attached to the noun-frame *<node>* to form the case-frame *<which-node>*, which is then placed on *buff*.

(s4) ⟶

s5. {[*frames* *nil*]
[*buff* <S> <at-5-ns> <which-node>]
[*vbuff* *nil*]
[*sconf* 10]}

Is: *<At-5-ns>* is placed on the *case-fills:* slot of the verb-frame *<be>* as the filler of the *temporal* case-role. Since *<at-5-ns>* is an optional case-role filler, the confidence-level is decreased by 4 (see Section 5.6.1). *<Which-node>* is placed on the *pending:* slot. (This slot then reads: *[pending: (x00001 pred p-locative *)]*.)

(s5) ⟶

s6. {[*frames* <be, <at-5-ns>, <which-node>>]
[*buff* <S>]
[*vbuff* *nil*]
[*sconf* 6]}

The: The determiner-frame *<the>* is placed on **buff**.

(s6) ⟶

s7. {[*frames* <be, <at-5-ns>, <which-node>>]
[*buff* <S> <the>]
[*vbuff* *nil*]
[*sconf* 6]}

Voltage: *<The>* is attached to the noun-frame *<voltage>* to form the case-frame *<the-voltage>*, which is then placed on **buff**.

(s7) ⟶

s8. {[*frames* <be, <at-5-ns>, <which-node>>]
[*buff* <S> <the-voltage>]
[*vbuff* *nil*]
[*sconf* 6]}

Maximum: *Maximum* is recognized both as an adjective and as a noun, and, correspondingly, two parse-states are instantiated. In the latter case, *maximum* is considered to be a count-noun, and since it is not preceded by a determiner, the confidence-level of this latter parse-state is reduced. The adjective interpretation does not force the attachment of *<the-voltage>*; the noun interpretation does.

(s8) ⟶

s9. {[*frames* <be, <at-5-ns>, <which-node>>]
[*buff* <S> <the-voltage> <maximum$_{adj}$>]
[*vbuff* *nil*]
[*sconf* 6]}

s10. {[*frames* <be, <at-5-ns>, <which-node>,
<the-voltage>>]
[*buff* <S> <maximum>]
[*vbuff* *nil*]
[*sconf* 4]}

At: State *(s9)* is recognized as incorrect since an adjective cannot be followed by a preposition. In state *(s10)*, the *pending:* slot of the verb-frame is searched for a case-frame with an asterisk included in its list of possible case-roles, and *<which-node>* is found. The attachment of *<at>* to *<which-node>* succeeds, and a parse-state representing a *wh*-fronted interpretation is instantiated. In this parse-state, *<maximum>* is attached to the verb-frame as the filler of the *pred* case-role. An alternative parse-state is also instantiated in which the preposition is simply placed on **buff**, in expectation of a following noun-phrase. The confidence-levels of both parse-states are reduced in this process.

(s10) ⟶

s11. {[*frames* <be,<at-5-ns>,<the-voltage>,<maximum>,
<at-which-node>]
[*buff* <S>]
[*vbuff* *nil*]
[*sconf* -1]}

s12. {[*frames* <be, <at-5-ns>, <which-node>,
<the-voltage>>]
[*buff* <S> <maximum> <at>]
[*vbuff* *nil*]
[*sconf* 2]}

?: State *(s12)* is terminated since its top **buff** element is neither a case-frame nor a clause-boundary-marker. Instantiating the final parse-state in the context of state *(s11)* is a straightforward matter of closing the only verb-frame.

(s11) ⟶

s13. {[*frames* <be,<at-5-ns>,<the-voltage>,<maximum>,
<at-which-node>]
[*buff* *nil*]
[*vbuff* *nil*]
[*sconf* -1]}

In this example, the resolution of the *wh*-fronting was facilitated by there being only one preposition after the *wh* noun phrase. Cleopatra will also correctly interpret such sentences as *Which node is the voltage maximum at 5 ns at?* and *Which node is the voltage maximum at at 5 ns?* although in both these cases a few more parse-states will be instantiated.

6.3. Example 3

For a last example, we examine a sentence with a subordinate clause. The subordinate clause here is in fact a headless relative clause (see Section 5.2.4), and tense information has to be utilized to distinguish the main from the subordinate clause.

S32. When does the voltage at n1 exceed 3 volts when the voltage at n2 equals 5 volts?

In our analysis of this sentence, we ignore the "linear" interpretation of *NP-PP* compounds such as *the voltage at n1.* (For faster response time, the linear interpretation is normally disabled when the *NP* is a function-noun and the *PP* an argument-noun, though this disabling is effected by a manipulation of confidence-levels in a manner not shown below.)

When: The pronoun-frame *<when>* is placed on **buff**.

```
s1.   {[*frames*  nil]
       [*buff*    <S> <when>]
       [*vbuff*   <S'>]
       [*sconf*   10]}
```

Does: *Does* is just a tense marker. A *tns:* slot is added to *<S'>* with the value *pres*.

(s1) →

```
s2.   {[*frames*  nil]
       [*buff*    <S> <when>]
       [*vbuff*   <S'>]
       [*sconf*   10]}
```

The: The determiner-frame *<the>* is placed on **buff**.

(s2) →

```
s3.   {[*frames*  nil]
       [*buff*    <S> <when> <the>]
       [*vbuff*   <S'>]
       [*sconf*   10]}
```

Voltage: *<The>* is attached to the noun-frame *<voltage>* to form the case-frame *<the-voltage>*, which is then placed on **buff**. The presence of a *tns:* slot-value in *<S'>* keeps the headless relative clause interpretation from being considered.

(s3) →

```
s4.   {[*frames*  nil]
       [*buff*    <S> <when> <the-voltage>]
       [*vbuff*   <S'>]
       [*sconf*   10]}
```

At: The preposition-frame *<at>* is placed on **buff**.

(s4) →

```
s5.   {[*frames*  nil]
       [*buff*    <S> <when> <the-voltage> <at>]
       [*vbuff*   <S'>]
       [*sconf*   10]}
```

N1: *<At>* is attached to the noun-frame *<n1>* to form the case-frame *<at-n1>*. A relative-clause is instantiated with *<the-voltage>* as its head (see Section 5.2.2).

(s5) ⟶

s6. {[*frames* <be, <^the-voltage>>]
[*buff* <S> <when> <the-voltage>
<S_r> <at-n1>]
[*vbuff* <S'>]
[*sconf* 10]}

Exceed: *<At-n1>* is attached to the relative-clause verb-frame which is then closed. Both *<the-voltage>* and *<when>* are attached to the new verb-frame *<exceed>*. Another interpretation is also attempted in which *<at-n1>* would be attached to *<exceed>*, but the attempted closing of the relative-clause verb-frame, a necessary condition for this interpretation, fails since there is then no filler for the *pred* case-role of the relative-clause verb-frame.

(s6) ⟶

s7. {[*frames* <be, <^the-voltage>, <at-n1>>
<exceed, <the-voltage>, <when>>]
[*buff* <S>]
[*vbuff* *nil*]
[*sconf* 10]}

3: The noun-frame *<3>* is placed on *buff*.

(s7) ⟶

s8. {[*frames* <be, <^the-voltage>, <at-n1>>
<exceed, <the-voltage>, <when>>]
[*buff* <S> <3>]
[*vbuff* *nil*]
[*sconf* 10]}

Volts: A *units:* slot is added to the case-frame *<3>* with the value *volts.*

(s8) →

```
s9.   {[*frames*  <be, <^the-voltage>, <at-n1>>
                  <exceed, <the-voltage>, <when>>]
       [*buff*    <S> <3-v>]
       [*vbuff*   nil]
       [*sconf*   10]}
```

When: The pronoun-frame *<when>* is placed on **buff**.

(s9) →

```
s10.  {[*frames*  <be, <^the-voltage>, <at-n1>>
                  <exceed,<the-voltage>,<when>,<3-v>>]
       [*buff*    <S> <when>]
       [*vbuff*   nil]
       [*sconf*   10]}
```

The: The determiner-frame *<the>* is placed on **buff**.

(s10) →

```
s11.  {[*frames*  <be, <^the-voltage>, <at-n1>>
                  <exceed,<the-voltage>,<when>,<3-v>>]
       [*buff*    <S> <when> <the>]
       [*vbuff*   nil]
       [*sconf*   10]}
```

Voltage: The occurrence of the *wh* case-frame *<when>* and the case-frame *<the-voltage>* without an intervening tense-marker triggers the headless-relative-clause analysis (see Section 5.2.4). The "linear" interpretation is not pursued since it requires both *<when>* case-frames, both of which must of course fill the *temporal* case-role, to be attached to one verb-frame. (In fact, multiple *temporal* case-role fillers are accepted under certain conditions; if both are *<when>* case-frames, one must be a relative-clause head.)

(s11) →

s12. {[*frames* <be, <^the-voltage$_1$>, <at-n1>>
<exceed,<the-voltage$_1$>,<when>,<3-v>>]
[*buff* <S> <when>
<S$_r$> <^when> <the-voltage$_2$>]
[*vbuff* <S$_r$'>]
[*sconf* 8]}

At: The preposition-frame *<at>* is placed on **buff**.

(s12) →

s13. {[*frames* <be, <^the-voltage$_1$>, <at-n1>>
<exceed,<the-voltage$_1$>,<when>,<3-v>>]
[*buff* <S> <when>
<S$_r$> <^when> <the-voltage$_2$> <at>]
[*vbuff* <S$_r$'>]
[*sconf* 8]}

N2: *<At>* is attached to the noun-frame *<n2>* to form the case-frame *<at-n2>*. A relative-clause is instantiated.

(s13) →

s14. {[*frames* <be, <^the-voltage$_1$>, <at-n1>>
<exceed,<the-voltage$_1$>,<when>,<3-v>>
<be, <^the-voltage$_2$>>]
[*buff* <S> <when>
<S_r> <^when> <the-voltage$_2$>
<S_{r2}> <at-n2>]
[*vbuff* <S_r'>]
[*sconf* 8]}

Equals: *Equals* has two morphemes. First the present tense morpheme is processed, which leads to a parse-state in which a *tns:* slot-value is added to <S_r'> to indicate present tense. This parse-state is notationally identical to state *(s14)* above.

(s14) →

s15. {[*frames* <be, <^the-voltage$_1$>, <at-n1>>
<exceed,<the-voltage$_1$>,<when>,<3-v>>
<be, <^the-voltage$_2$>>]
[*buff* <S> <when>
<S_r> <^when> <the-voltage$_2$>
<S_{r2}> <at-n2>]
[*vbuff* <S_r'>]
[*sconf* 8]}

Next, the root-verb morpheme is processed. *<At-n2>* is attached to the open relative-clause verb-frame, which is then closed. Both *<the-voltage$_2$>* and *<^when>* are attached to the new verb-frame *<equal>*, and the tense information from <S_r'> is incorporated. *<Equal>* is placed on **frames**. An alternative interpretation is also attempted, but this interpretation requires the closing of the open relative-clause verb-frame without the attachment of *<at-n2>* to it. The failure of this closing aborts the interpretation.

(s15) →

s16. {[*frames* <be, <^the-voltage$_1$>, <at-n1>>
<exceed,<the-voltage$_1$>,<when>,<3-v>>
<be, <^the-voltage$_2$>, <at-n2>>
<equal,<the-voltage$_2$>,<^when>>]
[*buff* <S> <when> <S$_r$>]
[*vbuff* *nil*]
[*sconf* 4]}

5: The noun-frame <*5*> is placed on **buff**.

(s16) →

s17. {[*frames* <be, <^the-voltage$_1$>, <at-n1>>
<exceed,<the-voltage$_1$>,<when>,<3-v>>
<be, <^the-voltage$_2$>, <at-n2>>
<equal,<the-voltage$_2$>,<^when>>]
[*buff* <S> <when> <S$_r$> <5>]
[*vbuff* *nil*]
[*sconf* 4]}

Volts: A *units:* slot is added to <*5*> with the value *volts*.

(s17) →

s18. {[*frames* <be, <^the-voltage$_1$>, <at-n1>>
<exceed,<the-voltage$_1$>,<when>,<3-v>>
<be, <^the-voltage$_2$>, <at-n2>>
<equal, <the-voltage$_2$>, <^when>>]
[*buff* <S> <when> <S$_r$> <5-v>]
[*vbuff* *nil*]
[*sconf* 4]}

9: The case-frame *<5-v>* is attached to *<equal>* (alternative attachments do not work since *<equal>* cannot otherwise be closed). The relative-clause head *<when>* is attached to the main-verb frame *<exceed>*. Note that *<exceed>* has two temporal case-role fillers (the earlier *<when>* and this later one). However, such multiple attachments are permitted under certain conditions, the relevant one here being that one of the case-fillers be a relative-clause head. There is one final parse-state:

(s18) ⟶

s19. {[*frames* <be, <^the-voltage$_1$>, <at-n1>>
<exceed, <the-voltage$_1$>, <when>,
<3-v>, <when>>
<be, <^the-voltage$_2$>, <at-n2>>
<equal,<the-voltage$_2$>,<^when>,<5-v>>]
[*buff* *nil*]
[*vbuff* *nil*]
[*sconf* 2]}

Note that in this example no ambiguity was manifested (but recall that we have not indicated the "linear" interpretations of complex noun phrases such as *the voltage at n1*). If we had fronted the headless relative clause (i.e. if the example sentence had been *When the voltage at n2 equals 5 v when does the voltage at n1 exceed 3 v?*) Cleopatra would have carried along two parallel interpretations until the word *does* was read, at which point the tense information would have aborted the interpretation in which the first clause was assumed to be an (ungrammatical) main-clause.

The sentences we have examined in this chapter are atypical in one sense: the parallelism exhibited in their parsings is relatively small. Considerations of space have also kept us from exemplifying the full variety of constructions that Cleopatra can handle. Nevertheless, these examples should have shed sufficient light on any remaining mysteries of Cleopatra's parsing process to enable the reader to work out how other sentences we have encountered in our discussion of Cleopatra's capabilities would be parsed, and how further constructions could be implemented.

In a natural language interface, of course, it is not enough just to parse a sentence. A response has to be computed too, and it is to this topic that we now turn.

Chapter 7
Semantic Interpretation

We turn our attention in this chapter from the parsing process to the semantic interpretation process. After the final parse-state has been derived, the semantic interpretation process computes the answer to the query. In the process of computing this answer, the circuit-simulator output will usually be accessed.[21] The semantic interpreter has to determine, from the augmented case-frame representation of the parse-state, both the node and time parameters for the required simulation values, and the operations (if any) that need to be performed on these values.

We first outline the semantic interpretation process, and then show evaluation procedures for a verb-frame and a case-frame. We do not discuss answer *presentation* (i.e. the format of the answer as the user sees it) in this chapter.

---

[21]It is only for "calculator" questions (such as *What is 2 plus 3?*) that accessing the simulation output is not necessary.

7.1. An Outline of the Semantic Interpretation Process

Each verb-frame has an *eval:* slot that names the evaluation procedure specific to that verb. The *lf:* slot serves the corresponding function in case-frames. (The evaluation procedure for a case-frame is the evaluation procedure for the head noun of the case-frame.) The interpretation process is recursive, the recursion mirroring the nestings of frames in the parse-state. The process is initiated by finding the verb-frame for the main-verb. The evaluation procedure for this verb-frame is then executed. In the evaluation procedure for a verb-frame, the case-frames that fill case-roles may be evaluated. If a case-frame is a simple noun phrase or prepositional phrase, the evaluation consists usually of executing the procedure specified in the *lf:* slot of the case-frame. However, a case-frame could also be an adverbial clause or the head of a relative-clause. The evaluation of such a case-frame requires the evaluation of the verb-frame for the adverbial or relative clause, and so on. For example, the query *What is the voltage at n1?* has *be* as its main-verb. The evaluation procedure for the associated verb-frame will require the evaluation of its *subj* role case-filler. This filler, however, is *<the-voltage>*, a relative-clause head (see Section 5.2.2). The call to evaluate *<the-voltage>* will result in the evaluation of the relative-clause verb. (Since the relative-clause verb is also *be*, the same evaluation-procedure will be invoked for the relative-clause that was invoked for the main clause.)

Frames are not evaluated independently of each other. The parsing process ensures that locative and time information is attached to the highest possible verb-frame, and the semantic interpretation process ensures that this information is inherited by embedded frames. For example, in the query *Is the voltage at n1 greater than the voltage at n2 at 5 ns?* the *temporal* case-role filler (*<at-5-ns>*) will be attached to the main-verb. This time-specification is inherited by the lower-level frames. Cleopatra will not waste time retrieving the voltages at nodes *n1* and *n2* at all time-points; only the voltage at *n1* at 5 ns and the voltage at *n2* at 5 ns will be retrieved.

7.2. Examples

7.2.1. Case-Frame Evaluations

An evaluation procedure usually returns a list. The first element of the list is a symbol that identifies the list as a set of voltage values, node identifiers, time points and intervals, or cardinal numbers. For voltage value lists, the other elements of the list will be lists too, specifying nodes, times, and the values. For lists of node identifiers, time points and intervals, and cardinal numbers, the second (and last) element will list the node identifers, time specification, and cardinal numbers, respectively. We give below some examples of the values returned by the evaluation procedures for specific case-frames:

<at-5-ns> (tloc: (5))
Tloc is short for *time-locative.*

<after-5-ns> (tloc: ((5 . 25)))
The particular simulation output file being accessed here has 25 ns as the final time-point. The dotted pair notation denotes a time-interval.

<and, <at-5-ns>, <after-15-ns>>
(tloc: (5 (15 . 25)))
Time-points and time-intervals can be intermingled.

<5-ns-after-the-voltage-at-n1-reaches-5-v>

(tloc: (11))
The voltage at *n1* reaches 5 volts at 6 ns. The presence of the prefix converts a time-interval into a time-point.

<at-n1>

(ploc: (!nodes n1))
Ploc is short for *physical-locative.* Nodes are considered to be points in space.

<the-voltage-at-n1-at-5-ns>

(!voltage (ploc: (!nodes n1)) (tloc: (5)) (values: (4.0)))

<the-voltages-at-n1-and-n2-at-5-ns>

(!voltage (ploc: (!nodes n1 n2)) (tloc: (5) (5)) (values: (4.0) (0.0)))

<the-voltages-at-n1-at-5-and-10-ns>

(!voltage (ploc: (!nodes n1)) (tloc: (5 10)) (values: (4.0 5.0)))

<and, <at-n1>, <n2>>

(ploc: (!nodes n1 n2))

<than-5-v>

(!cardinal (values: (5)))

<when>

(tloc:)

<what>

?
(*sic*)

Case-frames such as *<greater>*, *<average>*, *<maximum>*, and *<sum>* are not evaluated. These case-frames specify operations to be performed on other case-frames, and the nature of these operations can be ascertained from the *value:* slots of these (operator) case-frames.

7.2.2. The evaluation procedure for *<be>*

1. Get the *subj*, *pred*, *p-locative*, *temporal*, and *comparand* case-fillers. (Not all these case-fillers need be present. The *p-locative* case-role refers to nodes.)

2. If the *p-locative* filler is present, then evaluate the filler and assert the returned value as locative information.

3. If the *temporal* filler is present, then evaluate the filler and assert the returned value as temporal information.

4. If at least one of the following conditions are satisfied:

   a. *<Pred>* has *adj-pred* on its *type:* slot. (*<Pred>* refers to the case-frame that fills the *pred* case-role.)

   b. *<Pred>* has *number* on its *type:* slot, and *<subj>* has *arith-function* on its *features:* slot.

   c. *<Pred>* has *between* on its *type:* slot (when a case-frame is a prepositional phrase, the name of the preposition is indicated on the case-frame's *type:* slot), has *quantity* on its *features:* slot, and does not have *arg-for-arith-function* on its *features:* slot. (The last clause differentiates between a sentence such as *When is the voltage at n1 between 2 and 3 volts?* and one such as *What is the difference between . . . ?* The latter will not trigger the following *then:* actions, and is instead handled in step 8.)

   then:

   a. If no locative information has been asserted, then assert the locative information, if any, from the parent (calling) frame.

b. If no temporal information has been asserted, then assert the temporal information, if any, from the parent frame.

c. Evaluate *<subj>* with the asserted locative and temporal information, if any.

d. Evaluate *<comparand>* with the asserted locative and temporal information, if any. (The *comparand* case is a prepositional phrase such as *than 3 volts.*)

e. If the *value:* slot-value of *<pred>* is *equal-to*, then return the part of the *<subj>* evaluation which represents time-points at which the *<subj>* evaluation is equal to the *<comparand>* evaluation.

   If the *value:* slot-value of *<pred>* is *greater-than*, then return the part of the *<subj>* evaluation which represents time-points at which the *<subj>* evaluation is greater than the *<comparand>* evaluation.

   If the *value:* slot-value of *<pred>* is *less-than*, then return the part of the *<subj>* evaluation which represents time-points at which the *<subj>* evaluation is less than the *<comparand>* evaluation.

   If *<pred>* has *between* on its *type:* slot, then evaluate *<pred>* with the asserted temporal and locative information, if any, and return the part of the *<subj>* evaluation which represents time-points at which the *<subj>* evaluation is between values specified by the *<pred>* evaluation.

   If *<pred>* has *number* on its *type:* slot, then evaluate *<pred>* with the asserted temporal and locative information, if any, and return the part of the *<subj>*

evaluation which represents time-points at which the *<subj>* evaluation is equal to the *<pred>* evaluation. (*When is the voltage at n1 5 volts?* is treated as synonymous with *When is the voltage at n1 equal to 5 volts?*)

If *<pred>* has *maximum*, *greatest*, or *highest* on its *value:* slot, then return the part of the *<subj>* evaluation which represents the time-point(s) at which the *<subj>* evaluation is highest.

If *<pred>* has *minimum*, *least*, or *lowest* on its *value:* slot, the return the part of the *<subj>* evaluation which represents the time-point(s) at which the *<subj>* evaluation is lowest.

5. If *<pred>* does not have *location* on its *features:* slot, and no locative information has been asserted as yet, then assert locative information, if any, from the parent frame.

6. If *<pred>* does not have *t-value* on its *features:* slot, and no temporal information has been asserted as yet, then assert temporal information, if any, from the parent frame.

7. Evaluate *<pred>* with the asserted locative and temporal information, if any. (The evaluation of *<pred>* may itself return locative or temporal information, in which case this locative or temporal information will be asserted as such.)

8. If *<subj>* has *arith-function* on its *features:* slot, then:

   a. If *<subj>* is a relative-pronoun whose head has *sum* as its *value:* slot-value, then return the sum of the parameters represented by the *<pred>* evaluation. (*<Pred>* could represent *the voltages at n1 and n2*, for instance.)

If the head-value is *difference*, then return the difference.

If the head-value is *product*, then return the product.

9. If *<subj>* has *existential-there* as its *pos:* slot-value, then return the *<pred>* evaluation.

10. Evaluate *<subj>* with the asserted temporal and locative information, if any, and return the result. (For example, *<subj>* could be *<the-voltage>*, or, more precisely, *<ˆthe-voltage>*. The locative information will specify the nodes for which voltage-values are required, and the temporal information will specify the time-points at which the node-voltage-values are required.)

7.2.3. The evaluation procedure for *<voltage>*

If a *<the-voltage>* case-frame is a relative-clause head, this evaluation procedure is not invoked by the case-frame directly. Instead, the relative-clause verb is found and *its* evaluation procedure is executed. Within this evaluation procedure, the relative pronoun case-frame will require evaluation. Since a relative pronoun case-frame inherits its *lf:* slot from its head case-frame, the evaluation of the relative pronoun case-frame *<ˆthe-voltage>* will result in the invocation of this evaluation procedure.

1. If the locative information asserted by the parent frame is a node specification, then store it as such. If no locative information is asserted by the parent frame, or if the locative information is not a node specification, then assert all the simulated nodes as the node specification. (A circuit simulation usually traces the voltages at a few of the many nodes in a circuit.)

2. If there is temporal information asserted by the parent frame, then store it as the time specification. Otherwise assert the entire time span of the simulation as the time specification.

3. If there is just one node in the node specification, then retrieve the voltage values for that node at the time points and intervals specified by the time specification.

   Else retrieve the voltage values for each node at the time points and intervals specified by the time specification, and conjoin them.

4. If the case-frame has *adjectivized* on its *features:* slot (this feature may be inherited), then:

   a. Retrieve the adjective-frame. (This will require accessing the head case-frame if the *adjectivized* feature was inherited. The semantic interpretation process cannot handle multiple adjectives modifying the same noun.)

   b. If the adjective-frame has *average* on its *value:* slot, then compute the average(s) of the values computed in step 3.

      If the adjective-frame has *maximum* on its *value:* slot, then compute the maximum(s) of the values computed in step 3.

      If the adjective-frame has *minimum* on its *value:* slot, then compute the minimum(s) of the values computed in step 3.

   c. Return the new values, appropriately formatted.

5. Return the values computed in step 3.

This substantially concludes our exposition of how Cleopatra processes English queries. In the next chapter we will discuss some features of Cleopatra that help make it a usable (and extendable) CAD tool. The input and output formats can be gleaned from Appendix A, which is the transcript of a sample terminal session with Cleopatra, and in Appendix B we describe in detail how a particular extension was implemented—the ability to handle imperative constructions such as *Display the voltage at n1.*

Chapter 8
Issues for Further Research

The breadth and complexity of the CAD domain stands in sharp contrast to the limited domains of previous natural language interfaces. Unlike most previous work on natural language interfaces, in which there could be reasonable hope that a first implementation would be essentially complete, our ambitions prescribe incremental development of Cleopatra. Another consequence of the diversity of the CAD domain is that we cannot predict, a priori, what changes and enhancements future extensions of domain and analysis of "real" use might necessitate.

The generality and power of our approach has not only yielded Cleopatra's present abilities; just as importantly, it has provided a framework within which future extensions of domain, and whatever other improvements usage over time might suggest, should be greatly facilitated. We have attempted to ensure that Cleopatra can easily achieve further linguistic sophistication, and that the facilities exist to augment Cleopatra's "user-friendliness."

In this chapter we discuss some topics for future research. Our emphasis will be on extensions in functionality. In particular, we will discuss the improvements needed in order to use Cleopatra as a natural language interface for other domains and in order to make Cleopatra a "robust" interface. The last section of this chapter capsules the issue of experimental validation, which is in some sense orthogonal to the functionality issue.

8.1. Extending Cleopatra to Other Domains

One obvious topic for future work is broadening Cleopatra's domain of application, especially to other domains within CAD. The extensions that Cleopatra would need in order to function as a natural language interface for some other domain are of two types: the new domain may require the handling of some constructions that have not been implemented, and the domain-specific parts of Cleopatra will need to be rewritten. In this section, we discuss some candidate constructions, and how portable the various components of Cleopatra are.

8.1.1. Linguistic Extensions

Another sub-domain of CAD which we are certain would profit from a natural language interface is *behavioral* simulation post-processing—instead of reading a *SPICE* output file, Cleopatra would read an *ISPS*-simulator output-file [2]. The behavioral-simulation post-processing sub-domain is similar to Cleopatra's present sub-domain (circuit-simulation post-processing), but it differs enough in some relevant details to require the handling of some further constructions.

Cleopatra's linguistic abilities are, in general, not domain-specific. In fact, some constructions that Cleopatra can handle currently are of little use in the circuit-simulation post-processing sub-domain. For example, we doubt if much use will be made of the *there*-insertion construction in the present version of Cleopatra. For an *ISPS*-simulation, on the other hand, the ability to phrase questions such as the following would undoubtedly be useful:

S33. Is there a condition-code register bit that is asserted after the second clock cycle?

There are other constructions, of even less use in the present domain, which are not fully implemented but the rudiments of which are present. Recall, for example, our mention of noun-groups in the integration procedure for nouns (Section 4.3.1), and of relative clauses under relative-pronoun-deletion (Section 5.2.3). A designer using a natural language interface for behavioral simulation post-processing could be expected to avail himself of these constructions frequently.

There is a class of expressions which is of substantial importance in most domains but which some peculiarities of the circuit-simulation post-processing sub-domain has enabled us to ignore to this point. We refer to anaphoric expressions, and especially pronouns.

There are two reasons why we chose not to attempt pronoun-comprehension. First of all, there are few occasions to use pronouns in a domain with such a paucity of "objects" to which pronominal reference could be made, and on many of these occasions ellipsis is equally natural and more economical of effort:

> What is the voltage at n1 at 5 ns?
>
> What is it at 10 ns?

> What is the voltage at n1 at 5 ns?
>
> At 10 ns?

(This is not to say that pronouns are useless in our present domain; there is no elliptic variant of *What is the voltage at n1?* followed by *When is it greater than 2 volts?*)

The second reason is that the domain of circuit-simulation post-processing does not provide an adequate testbed for pronoun-resolution. The difficult (and interesting) problem in pronoun handling is resolving the referent of the pronoun. In general there can be many candidates for the referent of a pronoun. In this domain, however, there is rarely any potential ambiguity, and therefore the generality of a pronoun-handling capability implemented for this domain would be problematic.

A domain such as behavioral-simulation post-processing, on the other hand, is rich in objects to which pronominal reference could be made. A designer could follow up on sentence *(S33)* by asking either of the following questions (note that the referents of the two pronouns are different):

> After the third one?
>
> Is there any other one?

One prerequisite for pronoun-resolution is a "focus" data-structure that lists the case-frames that are recent enough to be possible referents for pronouns. This data-structure should also indicate the rankings of these case-frames as candidates for reference. These rankings would be functions of the position within a sentence of a case-frame (such as whether a case-frame was sentence-initial or not, or whether it was in the main-clause or in a subordinate-clause), and of the recency and frequency of prior pronominal reference, to give three factors.

The "focus" data-structure would have to be a parse-state variable; it could not be a global variable, updated after each sentence, since a pronoun can refer to a phrase in the same sentence:

> Is the first bit of the register 0 and the second one 1?

Given focus information, Cleopatra's parallelism should greatly facilitate dealing with referential ambiguity. A separate parse-state could be instantiated for each possible referent, and the confidence-level of a parse-state could reflect the ranking of that referent. Since pronouns can precede their referents too, we could instantiate an extra parse-state whenever a pronoun is encountered. In this parse-state the referent-link in the pronoun-frame would be absent initially; as further case-frames are composed the pronoun can be linked to them. Of course, the constraint-testing routines would need to be modified to deal with delayed referent identification. (Constraints and features would be inherited for preceding referents, as is done with features for relative-pronouns at present.)

There is a great deal of work on anaphora that should prove helpful when we attempt pronoun comprehension in Cleopatra (In particular, see [35, 68, 56]. Hirst provides a comprehensive review of anaphora-resolution techniques in [40].)

8.1.2. Portability Considerations

Once such enhancements as pronoun-comprehension and intra-sentential ellipsis (which we discuss in the following section) are incorporated into Cleopatra, and to a limited extent even in its present state, Cleopatra could be ported not only to other sub-domains within CAD, but also to technical domains not related to VLSI design. For each new domain, of course, some customization will be necessary.

There is a fairly clean distinction in Cleopatra's architecture between the parsing component and the semantic interpretation component. The semantic interpretation component would need to be tailored for each new domain. One general semantic interpretation procedure for all domains is a long-term aspiration; even with a general parsing component, the user could initially be forced to indicate context-changes explicitly so that the right semantic component could be loaded in. We should remark that the semantic interpretation process for most domains is more involved than for our present domain. For example, querying complex data-bases[22] in natural language is likely to produce ambiguities of quantifier-scoping. Such ambiguities could only be detected by the semantic interpretation procedure (at present all ambiguities are detected in the parsing procedure).

We can also think of the parsing component as separable into the dictionary, as represented by the lexical and dictionary entries, and the parser proper, as represented by the integration procedures. Since every technical domain has its own vocabulary, a new set of lexical and dictionary entries would need to be composed for each, although some common words such as determiners and verbal auxiliaries would not need any redefinition, and others such as prepositions and the verbs *be* and *have* would require little more than the reworking of their constraint slots. The degree of coupling between the dictionary and the integration procedures is greater than that between the parsing component and the semantic interpretation component, and it might take a few debugging iterations before some information in dictionary entries (notably the *features:* slot-values) is finalized.

The integration procedures should be substantially portable to other domains without modification. The only significant domain-dependencies are confined to the confidence-level updating procedure for conjunctions and to the ellipsis-evaluation procedure, and adding a *category:* slot to case-frames (with some additional machinery) would remove the domain-dependencies therein (see p. 88).

---

[22] A circuit-simulation output-file can be considered a degenerate data-base.

8.2. Robustness

Robustness refers to the appropriate treatment of unorthodox input in an interface, and, therefore, largely determines the "user-friendliness" of the interface. How well a natural language interface can cope with elliptic input, with misspelt words, with "terse" expressions, and with ungrammaticality, are all factors that contribute to the robustness of the interface, and Cleopatra is wanting in each to some extent. However, the prospects for improvement are promising.

We have already dealt with Cleopatra's processing of ellipsis at some length (see Sections 5.5 and 5.6.3). To recapitulate the earlier discussion, Cleopatra allows one or more case-roles of a verb-frame from the previous sentence to be filled by new case-frames. Thus ellipsis in Cleopatra is limited to inter-sentential nominal substitutions. This is typical of most case-frame parsers, and is probably adequate for natural language interfaces that are used mostly for querying in technical domains. However, an intra-sentential ellipsis resolution ability would be helpful even in our present domain (see the example on p. 84).

Intra-sentential ellipsis resolution requires an ability to identify the particular case-frame that is responsible for a failed parse, and to locate a previous complex case-frame in the sentence which has as one component a case-frame similar to that particular case-frame. Cleopatra has a facility to identify causes of failure (we discuss this facility later in this section), and the case-frames on **buff**, as well as those attached to verb-frames on **frames**, can all be examined in an integration procedure to find an appropriate match.

If Cleopatra encounters a token that does not have an associated lexical procedure, that is not a node-identifier, and that is not a number, there may be either of two possible explanations: The first possibility is that the token is a misspelling of a word that is in Cleopatra's vocabulary; the second is that the token is a (correctly spelt) word that is not in Cleopatra's vocabulary. Cleopatra does not recognize this distinction. No spelling correction is attempted at present. When confronted with such a token, Cleopatra asks the user to type in a replacement. In order to handle run-together words, the substitute can be null or it can be a list of words. The user is also given the option of aborting the query.

Spelling correction, especially in domains of limited vocabulary, is not a difficult problem, and we do not envisage any problems in linking an existing spelling correction program to Cleopatra.

Cleopatra does not attempt morphological analyses of words either.[23] Again, however, incorporating a morphological analysis module should not present any problems for the limited vocabularies we are concerned with.

Frequent technical communications between the same (human) interlocutors often results in the definition and frequent use of customized abbreviations. In a natural language interface for technical domains too, allowing the user to define his own abbreviations lends significantly to the usability of the interface. Cleopatra provides such an ability with certain limitations: the abbreviations have to be single symbols and they cannot be words already in Cleopatra's vocabulary. One desirable variation this prohibits is the parametrized abbreviation.

---

[23]Checking the beginning and ending segments of words to detect morphemes is called *morphological analysis*. Examples: *equal* + *-s*, *voltage* + *-s*, *in-* + *equal* + *-ity* + *-s*.

The user cannot define an abbreviation such as *vx n1* for *the voltage at n1* and have Cleopatra subsequently treat a phrase such as *vx n2* in analogous fashion. (The LADDER natural language interface [38] allowed the user this liberty.)

The syntax for defining abbreviations is rigid. The first symbol must be *.abbrev*, followed (after any number of spaces) by the name for the new abbreviation, followed (possibly after spaces again) by a list containing the words the abbreviation should expand to. Other systems have used a pseudo-natural language syntax; users to the LADDER system could use sentences such as *Define JFK like Kennedy*.

We would like to invoke the concept of *closure* to argue that a rigid syntax is better, at least in our case.[24] The closer that two abilities are perceived to be in function, the greater is the tendency to generalize from the presence of one ability to the assumed presence of the other. To take an extreme example, a natural language interface that accepted a sentence such as *When is the voltage at n1 greater than 2 volts?* but not *Is the voltage at n1 greater than 2 volts?* would be disregarding closure.

Defining abbreviations is a task that is sufficiently distinct from the querying task. We can anticipate that few users will be prone to over-generalize by attempting to perform the former task in natural language if it is clear that the natural language comprehension capability of the interface is limited to queries. On the other hand, allowing a meta-utterance such as defining abbreviations in natural language could frequently lead users to attempt other meta-utterances, such as questions

---

[24] In [71], *psychological closure* is defined as "the feeling of having completed a task." What we mean by "closure" here is the more general association of a task with other similar tasks.

about the system's abilities (*How can I define my own abbreviations?*) Rather than prohibit all but one kinds of meta-utterances, we have prohibited all. LADDER's coverage of meta-utterances was spotty; it allowed more than just abbreviation definition in natural language, but it did not allow questions such as the one above.

Users of a natural language interface cannot always be expected to use impeccable grammar. Violations of subject-verb agreement and elisions of articles are common deviations from text-book prose, and Cleopatra tolerates both. Cleopatra also tolerates the elision of most prepositions. The user could therefore adopt a form of "terse" expression, for example:

When is voltage n1 greater than voltage n2?

By defining a couple of abbreviations this could be further contracted to:

When is vn n1 $>$ vn n2?

Tolerance of such ungrammaticality is "hard-wired" into Cleopatra's integration procedures, and other deviant constructions can be similarly handled. The interesting problem, though, is reasoning about the possible causes of a failed parse, and attempting corrections on that basis. Cleopatra has a facility for logging messages when the preconditions for an interpretation are not met and an integration procedure is terminated. These messages could provide the information that a higher-level procedure would need to identify the errant constituents and to attempt rectification. It should be said though that one problem with all schemes for inferring the causes of a failed parse is that they tend to be computationally expensive, and Cleopatra may be no exception.

Cleopatra cannot deal with "real" ambiguity: multiple final parse-states with identical confidence-levels. Again, this is not a problem in our present domain, but it could be a problem in a larger domain or in one which requires frequent use of quantifiers. The (readily implementable) solution is to present the possible alternatives to the user and require him to select the intended interpretation. (Of course, multiple final parse-states with identical confidence-levels could also indicate that the confidence-level updating factors require adjustment.)

In contrast to conventional interfaces, an on-line help facility is not critically important in a natural language interface. Nevertheless, such a facility would be useful if the user had forgotten the abbreviations that he had defined, or (in the present domain) the relevant simulation parameters (the simulated nodes and the time-interval of the simulation). A help facility could also indicate in some fashion the vocabulary of the interface. There are few enough conceivable help requests, at least in our present domain, that a rigid syntax would not be particularly demanding of cognitive effort.

8.3. Experimental Validation

The final determinant of the worth of a user-interface, whether conventional or natural-language, is the evaluation it receives, both in the short-term and after extended use, from its intended users. Although it may seem that a negative evaluation of an imperfect, incomplete Cleopatra in no way reflects on the worth of our ultimate goal (the development of a natural language interface for an integrated design environment), it is unlikely that unusable intermediate versions of Cleopatra can lead to a usable final version.

An important topic for future research, therefore, is the experimental validation of Cleopatra. We intend to release Cleopatra to circuit designers in industry. The feedback these designers provide us will be invaluable not only to us (i.e. to Cleopatra's future development), but also to other researchers in user-interfaces for CAD, and to other researchers in natural language interfaces. There is a real dearth of experimental study of natural language interfaces, especially with expert professionals as subjects. It would be well worth the extra effort to conduct such a study carefully, and with attention to detail.

Chapter 9
Conclusion, and Afterthoughts

The development of Cleopatra is just the first step towards our ultimate goal of developing a natural language interface for the entire CAD domain. The generality and power of the approach embodied in Cleopatra provide grounds for optimism that our ultimate goal is achievable, particularly at the "parsing" level. We have had little trouble handling constructions that many natural language interfaces forbear.

However, a caveat is in order at the levels of "semantics" and "pragmatics." The larger the domain of application of an interface, the more important these higher levels are for natural language comprehension. We have had little to say about either of these, and much research will eventually have to be done before Cleopatra can deal with phenomena at these levels adequately. We would like to emphasize again, though, that our approach is much less constrained than past approaches have been, both in the kinds of operations we can perform, and in the sources of knowledge we can incorporate. This flexibility augurs well for the long-term future too.

Cleopatra is more than a vehicle to demonstrate the feasibility of our ultimate goal. It is a useful CAD tool that fills an immediate need. Almost any alternative to manual extraction of circuit-simulation values from circuit-simulator output-files would be welcome, and Cleopatra provides an alternative that requires little learning, has high functionality, and is "user-friendly." We are confident that experimental studies will confirm the utility of Cleopatra and the advantages that natural language interfaces hold for CAD.

To the best of our knowledge, Cleopatra is the first natural language interface for a CAD domain. We anticipate that many others will be developed in the near future by other researchers in user-interfaces for CAD. Cleopatra may be a harbinger of a new era for the VLSI designer.

9.1. Afterthoughts

We have been looking at natural language understanding from an Artificial Intelligence perspective (one might label this an "engineering" perspective). At this juncture, we would like to reverse this bias and contrast our approach with the "linguistic" approach to natural language understanding.[25] Although the goals of linguistic science are rather distinct from our goals, we can nevertheless anticipate a criticism of our approach on linguistic grounds. In the process of responding to this criticism, we hope to furnish a justification of our approach at a higher, more abstract level than that to which our discussion has hitherto been confined.

The criticism is a general one: Are we not guilty of "overkill" in our repeated emphases on flexibility, procedural encodings, etc.? Surely, the criticism goes, language is a structured phenomenon, and its computational simulation does not require the power of a Turing machine.

---

[25] We use the term "linguistics" to refer to the particular sub-discipline of linguistics which is of relevance here: theoretical linguistics, especially within the Chomskyan framework.

The Chomskyan argument that it must be possible to parse language with greater parsimony is based on learning: Children learn their native languages in finite time, with finite data, and without being taught the "rules" of grammar explicitly [15]. Discovering a necessary and sufficient[26] (and thereby psychologically plausible) parsing mechanism for natural languages is a central concern of modern theoretical linguistics. However, the variety of theories within linguistics (for example, Lexical-Functional Grammar [42], Government-and-Binding [16], and Generalized Phrase Structure Grammar [31]), as well as the recency of these theories, attest to the facts that there is little agreement on this matter, and little hope for agreement in the near future. No single linguistic theory of currency is universally accepted.

But there is, and has been, substantial agreement between linguists on more general issues. Linguists have postulated constraints such as the "autonomy of syntax," the "competence-performance distinction," and the "literal-meaning hypothesis," which have enjoyed wide acceptance within the linguistic community. Such postulations may have made the linguist's inquiry tractable, but we would contend that their validity and usefulness are questionable.

In the mid-1960's, a strong version of the autonomy of syntax hypothesis was popular. It was assumed, *inter alia*, that semantic interpretation was completely independent of the choice of superficial syntactic form of a sentence [43, 14]. Thus in [14], the semantic interpretation process applied to an abstract representation of a sentence that was invariant of the "voice" of the sentence. However, Chomsky

---

[26] A death-knell of Transformational Grammar was the demonstration that every recursively enumerable set can be generated by a transformational grammar along Chomsky's *Aspects* model [58, 59].

himself proposed that some passive sentences differed in meaning from their active counterparts [13;pp.100-101, 14;p.224]. (According to Chomsky, *Every man in this room knows two languages* differs from *Two languages are known by every man in this room* in that the latter has the interpretation that each man knows the same two languages, while in the former the correct interpretation is that each man knows a different pair of languages.[27] Whether or not our intuitions agree with Chomsky's, we think it is correct to say that the *preferred* interpretations *are* different.) Katz and Postal [43], incidentally, presumed that corresponding active and passive structures did not have a common underlying representation, thereby abolishing one of the major original motivations for transformations [13;pp.42-43].

Further evidence against the mid-60's autonomy of syntax hypothesis is provided by Kiparsky and Kiparsky, who showed that the type of subordinate clause a verb takes can depend on certain semantic properties of the verb [45].

The "competence-performance" distinction [14] introduces a level of abstraction that distinguishes between language as we are consciously aware of it (called *performance*), and an idealized notion of linguistic knowledge that is neither accessible to introspection, nor directly manifested in verbal behavior (called *competence*). It is this latter notion of competence that is the object of the linguist's study. Consequently, linguists are not as concerned with describing *acceptable utterances* as they are concerned with describing *grammatical*

---

[27]Such differences of interpretation are not specific to active-passive pairs; they are specific to quantifier ordering. The same distinction can be made between *The teacher asked two questions of every student* and *The teacher asked every student two questions*. (But this is besides the point.)

sentences. A sentence such as *Oysters oysters oysters eat eat eat* would be considered grammatical, whereas *John and me had a long talk* would not!

There is a tension between, on the one hand, considering linguistic competence to be of psychological significance, and on the other, discounting all behavioral data (see [22;pp.332-335]). Pylyshyn, for example, resolves the tension by suggesting that theories of competence, while empirically and heuristically valid, have no psychological reality [62]. But to Chomsky, a grammar is "constructed at a given stage of mental growth" [15;p.53], and must thereby be psychologically real.

The problems of dealing with idioms and pragmatic phenomena such as indirect speech acts [64], has given rise to the "literal meaning hypothesis" (see, for example, [64] and [15]). According to this hypothesis, before recognizing the purpose or intent of the utterance of a sentence by the speaker, the hearer always computes the "literal meaning" of the sentence. Thus, on hearing a sentence such as *Can you reach the salt?* the hearer would first recognize this as being a yes-no question about his ability to reach the salt, and only then (by a further process of reasoning) recognize that the speaker was requesting him to pass the salt-container.

The literal meaning hypothesis is still widely accepted, but there is recent psychological evidence that argues strongly against it [61, 32]. It appears that hearers respond sooner when such questions are used idiomatically than when they are used literally. It is interesting to note that, although we make no claims for the psychological validity of our approach, we can indeed parse questions such as *Can you pass me the salt?* directly as requests. The "literal meaning" parse could also be carried along as a (weaker) alternative, and used only when the preconditions for the "indirect speech act" interpretation are not satisfied.

Finally, there are even cases where compositionality seems to break down, and no linguistic theory has an adequate explanation for that. Thus the sentence *John frightened sincerity* is nonsensical, but *One cannot say that John frightened sincerity* is not [14;pp.156-158].

Chomskyan linguistics is, of course, not the only discipline in which researchers have attempted to make difficult problems manageable by imposing structurings that the human mind is comfortable with. A great deal of work in artificial intelligence has also, we feel, suffered from poorly motivated attributions of regular structure to natural phenomena. For example, in [69], Simon discusses the complexity of human behavior:

> A man, viewed as a behaving system, is quite simple. The apparent complexity of his behavior over time is largely the result of the complexity of the environment in which he finds himself.

(This claimed simplicity is later explained as a consequence of hierarchical structure.)

Diametrically opposed to Chomsky and Simon are such philosophers as Hubert Dreyfus [22] and Wittgenstein (in his later period [78]), who contend that any "scientific" understanding of language or other aspects of human behavior is impossible. Wittgenstein, for example, despaired of a formal treatment of language use:

> §107. The more narrowly we examine actual language, the sharper becomes the conflict between it and our requirement. (For the crystalline purity of logic was, of course, not a *result of investigation*: it was a requirement.) (Italics in original.)

> §109. . . . We must do away with all *explanation*, and description alone must take its place. (Italics in original.)

Our views lie somewhere in between. On the one hand, we agree that cognitive ability (whether in the realm of language or problem-solving or some other aspect of human intelligence) must be innately and inherently constrained, and that it must therefore be subject, at least at some level, to formal explanation. However, we feel that it is not at all clear what these constraints are—the ones that modern-day theoretical linguists have proposed seem to be gross oversimplifications. In the light of our ignorance of the right set of constraints, we have followed what we feel is the logical alternative to the linguistic approach: to allow as much generality and power as possible in the underlying formalism, and not worry if this be more than is absolutely necessary (or minimally sufficient).

Appendix A
A Sample Session with Cleopatra

This appendix contains the annotated transcript of an actual terminal session with Cleopatra. A comparator was simulated with *SPICE*, and the *SPICE* output file (provided to us by David Lapotin) was read by Cleopatra. This particular simulation is not typical of simulations performed by designers in industry, which trace many more nodes for much longer periods of time. Our intention here, however, is less to illustrate how a designer can solve particular problems with Cleopatra, and more to demonstrate the range of constructions that he can use. The transcript also demonstrates the effective manner in which Cleopatra utilizes graphs and tables.

In the next section we show part of the output file, and then we present the transcript.

A.1. The *SPICE* Output File

We list below the relevant portion of the *SPICE* ouput file for our example circuit. Cleopatra obtains the time range of the simulation from the *.TRAN* statement, and the traced node-identifiers from the *.PRINT* statement. *SPICE* marks the beginning of the simulated values with an *X*, and the end with a *Y*.

```
.TRAN 0.5N 25N
.PRINT TRAN V(1), V(2), V(13), V(23), V(20), V(22), V(25)
.END
```

0**** TRANSIENT ANALYSIS TEMPERATURE = 27.000 DEG C

0**

TIME X	V(1)	V(2)	V(13)	V(23)	V(20)	V(22)	V(25)
0. e+00	0. e+00	0. e+00	5.000e+00	2.172e-07	2.172e-07	2.172e-07	5.000e+00
5.000e-10	0. e+00	0. e+00	5.000e+00	2.515e-07	9.083e-08	2.217e-07	5.000e+00
1.000e-09	0. e+00	0. e+00	5.000e+00	2.663e-07	9.730e-08	2.194e-07	5.000e+00
1.500e-09	5.000e-01	0. e+00	5.001e+00	1.348e-04	8.619e-05	-1.564e-07	5.000e+00
2.000e-09	1.000e+00	0. e+00	5.001e+00	8.923e-05	6.490e-05	-3.433e-07	5.000e+00
2.500e-09	1.500e+00	0. e+00	5.000e+00	-1.117e-05	2.118e-05	-3.245e-07	5.000e+00
3.000e-09	2.000e+00	0. e+00	5.000e+00	-1.311e-04	-2.293e-05	-1.703e-07	5.000e+00
3.500e-09	2.500e+00	0. e+00	4.999e+00	-2.787e-04	-1.309e-04	-4.258e-07	5.000e+00
4.000e-09	3.000e+00	0. e+00	4.997e+00	-8.926e-04	-3.206e-04	-8.064e-04	5.000e+00
4.500e-09	3.500e+00	0. e+00	4.995e+00	-1.941e-03	-5.864e-04	-2.363e-03	5.000e+00
5.000e-09	4.000e+00	0. e+00	4.992e+00	-2.990e-03	-8.522e-04	-3.920e-03	5.000e+00
5.500e-09	4.500e+00	0. e+00	4.993e+00	-4.235e-03	-6.579e-04	-7.573e-03	5.000e+00
6.000e-09	5.000e+00	0. e+00	4.996e+00	-5.628e-03	-1.176e-04	-1.280e-02	5.000e+00
6.500e-09	5.000e+00	0. e+00	5.022e+00	-3.362e-04	3.410e-03	-1.259e-02	5.000e+00
7.000e-09	5.000e+00	0. e+00	5.079e+00	1.283e-02	1.078e-02	-9.439e-03	5.001e+00
7.500e-09	5.000e+00	0. e+00	5.159e+00	2.887e-02	2.026e-02	-5.319e-03	5.001e+00
8.000e-09	5.000e+00	0. e+00	5.166e+00	2.567e-02	1.838e-02	-1.181e-03	5.001e+00
8.500e-09	5.000e+00	0. e+00	5.047e+00	-4.400e-03	-5.226e-04	1.768e-03	5.000e+00
9.000e-09	5.000e+00	0. e+00	4.807e+00	-5.564e-02	-3.379e-02	3.412e-03	4.997e+00
9.500e-09	5.000e+00	0. e+00	4.448e+00	-1.233e-01	-7.918e-02	3.876e-03	4.995e+00
1.000e-08	5.000e+00	0. e+00	4.035e+00	-1.796e-01	-1.206e-01	3.254e-03	4.993e+00
1.050e-08	5.000e+00	0. e+00	3.631e+00	-2.216e-01	-1.545e-01	2.312e-03	4.992e+00
1.100e-08	5.000e+00	0. e+00	3.269e+00	-2.179e-01	-1.615e-01	1.634e-03	4.993e+00
1.150e-08	5.000e+00	0. e+00	2.950e+00	-1.552e-01	-1.299e-01	1.831e-03	4.997e+00

1.200e-08	5.000e+00	0. e+00	2.657e+00	-4.626e-02	-7.130e-02	2.086e-03	5.002e+00
1.250e-08	5.000e+00	0. e+00	2.411e+00	1.515e-01	3.879e-02	2.380e-03	5.011e+00
1.300e-08	5.000e+00	0. e+00	2.166e+00	3.493e-01	1.489e-01	2.674e-03	5.019e+00
1.350e-08	5.000e+00	0. e+00	1.936e+00	6.420e-01	3.079e-01	2.804e-03	5.016e+00
1.400e-08	5.000e+00	0. e+00	1.752e+00	1.201e+00	6.045e-01	2.471e-03	4.980e+00
1.450e-08	5.000e+00	0. e+00	1.568e+00	1.761e+00	9.012e-01	2.139e-03	4.943e+00
1.500e-08	5.000e+00	0. e+00	1.384e+00	2.320e+00	1.198e+00	1.806e-03	4.907e+00
1.550e-08	5.000e+00	0. e+00	1.219e+00	2.857e+00	1.532e+00	1.549e-03	4.787e+00
1.600e-08	5.000e+00	0. e+00	1.108e+00	3.331e+00	1.972e+00	1.503e-03	4.429e+00
1.650e-08	5.000e+00	0. e+00	9.977e-01	3.804e+00	2.412e+00	1.457e-03	4.072e+00
1.700e-08	5.000e+00	0. e+00	8.872e-01	4.278e+00	2.852e+00	1.412e-03	3.714e+00
1.750e-08	5.000e+00	0. e+00	7.871e-01	4.650e+00	3.257e+00	1.375e-03	3.304e+00
1.800e-08	5.000e+00	0. e+00	7.163e-01	4.734e+00	3.562e+00	1.364e-03	2.746e+00
1.850e-08	5.000e+00	0. e+00	6.455e-01	4.819e+00	3.868e+00	1.353e-03	2.188e+00
1.900e-08	5.000e+00	0. e+00	5.768e-01	4.887e+00	4.147e+00	1.288e-03	1.678e+00
1.950e-08	5.000e+00	0. e+00	5.159e-01	4.888e+00	4.320e+00	1.018e-03	1.347e+00
2.000e-08	5.000e+00	0. e+00	4.550e-01	4.889e+00	4.494e+00	7.489e-04	1.017e+00
2.050e-08	4.500e+00	0. e+00	4.124e-01	4.911e+00	4.651e+00	3.343e-04	8.513e-01
2.100e-08	4.000e+00	0. e+00	3.709e-01	4.917e+00	4.748e+00	2.251e-04	6.405e-01
2.150e-08	3.500e+00	0. e+00	3.330e-01	4.925e+00	4.816e+00	3.067e-04	4.589e-01
2.200e-08	3.000e+00	0. e+00	2.993e-01	4.938e+00	4.866e+00	5.790e-04	3.326e-01
2.250e-08	2.500e+00	0. e+00	2.692e-01	4.950e+00	4.901e+00	9.483e-04	2.454e-01
2.300e-08	2.000e+00	0. e+00	2.439e-01	4.959e+00	4.925e+00	2.252e-03	1.858e-01
2.350e-08	1.500e+00	0. e+00	2.205e-01	4.968e+00	4.944e+00	3.885e-03	1.359e-01
2.400e-08	1.000e+00	0. e+00	1.979e-01	4.976e+00	4.963e+00	5.757e-03	8.884e-02
2.450e-08	5.000e-01	0. e+00	1.829e-01	4.982e+00	4.973e+00	1.031e-02	6.520e-02
2.500e-08	3.719e-15	0. e+00	1.596e-01	4.985e+00	4.979e+00	1.333e-02	4.756e-02

Y

A.2. The Session Transcript

In the following transcript, all user input is underlined, and all annotations are italicized. CPU times refer to the parsing process, not the actual data extraction and manipulation. (For the present example, the two are roughly comparable; for longer simulations, the data extraction would take much longer than the parsing. In every case, however, querying with Cleopatra would be significantly faster than manually going through the output listing.)

```
-> (cleo)
```

Cleopatra is invoked from FranzLisp.

```
SPICE output file: cleo.spice(cleo.spice read)
```

This is the SPICE output file of the previous section.

```
(nodes: n1 n2 n13 n23 n20 n22 n25)
(times: 0. . .25)
```

Cleopatra lists the node-identifiers that were defined for this simulation. The time-span of this simulation was from 0 to 25 ns.

```
>> (please enclose query in parentheses)
```

We would need to investigate how punctuation, especially commas, could be handled before removing this restriction. Furthermore, the parentheses allow queries to be longer than one line without requiring the user to signal the end of the query with some special code.

```
>> (when is the voltage at n1 greater than the voltage at n2)
. . . . . . . . . . . . . . (about 1 cpu second for 1 parse)
(volts)
5.328   |
4.995   |        ****************************
4.662   |       *                             *
4.329   |
3.996   |      *                               *
3.663   |     *                                 *
3.33    |
2.997   |    *                                   *
2.664   |   *                                     *
2.331   |
1.998   |  *                                       *
1.665   | *                                         *
1.332   |
0.999   | *                                          *
0.666   |*                                            *
0.333   |
0.0     |                                              *
         +----+----+----+----+----+----+----+----+----+
        1.5  4.0  6.5  9.0 11.5 14.0 16.5 19.0 21.5 24.0  (ns)

LEGEND:  * : n1
```

Cleopatra labels both axes automatically, and indicates the interpretation of the markers used for the graph.

```
>> (greater than the voltage at n13)
. . . . . . . (about 0 cpu second for 1 parse)
(volts)
5.162     |************************
4.829     |
4.496     |                        *
4.163     |                         *
3.83      |
3.497     |                          *
3.164     |                           *
2.831     |
2.498     |                            *
2.165     |                             *
1.832     |
1.499     |                              *
1.166     |                               *
0.833     |
0.5       |                                *
           +////+----+----+----+----+----+
          6.0 11.0 13.5 16.0 18.5 21.0 23.5  (ns)

LEGEND:  * : n1
```

*An example of ellipsis. This query is interpreted as "When is the voltage at n1 greater than the voltage at n13?" The slashes in the time-scale indicate a break. (The *'s corresponding to the slashes are misleading, and should be removed.)*

```
>> (less)
  (about 0 cpu second for 1 parse)
(volts)
5.328    |
4.995    |                                       *    *    *    *    *
4.662    |                                  *
4.329    |
3.996    |                             *
3.663    |                        *
3.33     |
2.997    |                   *
2.664    |              *
2.331    |
1.998    |         *
1.665    |    *
1.332    |
0.999    |                *
0.666    |           *
0.333    |
0.0      |*   *   *
          +-----+-----+-----+-----+-----+/////+-----+-----+
         0.0   1.0   2.0   3.0   4.0   5.0   6.5   7.5   8.5  (ns)

LEGEND:  * : n1
```

Interpreted as "When is the voltage at n1 less than the voltage at n13?"

```
>> (after the voltage at n1 reaches 3 v what is the maximum
        voltage at n13)
. . . . . . . . . . . . . . . . . . . (about 2 cpu seconds for  2 parses)
Node n13.  Time(s): (8.0)
   Voltage(s): (5.166)
```

This sentence has a fronted subordinate clause. With just one value to present, Cleoptra does not bother with a graph.

```
>> (what is the average voltage at n1 between 5 and 15 ns)
. . . . . . . . . . . . . . . (about 1 cpu second for  3 parses)
Node n1.  Time(s): ((5 . 15))
   Voltage(s): (4.928571428571429)
```

Here "average" is used as an adjective. "Between" is a preposition that requires a conjoined object. The dotted pair notation implies a time-interval, in this case from 5 ns to 15 ns.

```
>> (the minimum voltage)
. . . (about 0 cpu second for 1 parse)
Node n1.  Time(s): (5)
   Voltage(s): (4.0)
```

Interpreted as "What is the minimum voltage at n1 between 5 and 15 ns?"

```
>> (when is the voltage at n1 minimum)
. . . . . . . (about 0 cpu second for 1 parse)

        |      0.0 |      0.5 |      1.0 |      25.0 |
---------------------------------------------------------
     n1 |        0 |        0 |        0 | 3.719e-15 |
```

With between one and six time-points, Cleopatra selects a tabular format. In this sentence, "minimum" is used as a noun, not an adjective.

```
>> (maximum)
  (about 0 cpu second for 1 parse)
(volts)
5.1     |
5.0     |* * * * * * * * * * * * * * * * * * * * * * * * * * * *
         +---+---+---+---+---+---+---+---+---+---+---+---+---+---+
        6.0 7.0 8.0 9.010.011.012.013.014.015.016.017.018.019.020.0
                                                                  (ns)
 LEGEND:   * : n1
```

Interpreted as "When is the voltage at n1 maximum?"

```
>> (is there a node that has a voltage that is always less than
       3 v)
. . . . . . . . . . . . . . . . (about 0 cpu second for 1 parse)
Yes: (n2 n22)
```

A there-insertion sentence, a construction that is often a problem for case-frame parsers. Note also that this sentence contains an adverb and two relative clauses, one of which is nested inside the other.

```
>> (what are the voltages at n1 and n13 and n25 at 2.5 ns and
       after 15 ns)
. . . . . . . . . . . . . . . . . . . . (about 2 cpu seconds for  2
                                                  parses)
(volts)
5.328   |
4.995   |& x x x x x x x x x x
4.662   |  *                  x
4.329   |    *
3.996   |      *                x
3.663   |        *                x
3.33    |          *
2.997   |                           x
2.664   |            *                x
2.331   |              *
1.998   |                               x
1.665   |x               *                x
1.332   |  o               *
0.999   |    o o o           * *            x
0.666   |          o o o o o     *            x
0.333   |                    o o o & & & & o o o
0.0     |                                * * * &
         +///+---+---+---+---+---+---+---+---+---+
       2.516.017.018.019.020.021.022.023.024.0  25   (ns)

 LEGEND:  x : n1      o : n13      * : n25
```

The union of the temporal conjuncts is taken as the time-specification for this query. Cleopatra can draw multiple graphs, and it identifies each symbol when possible. The ampersands mark overlapping points. The scaling routines need some fine-tuning.

```
>> (between 20 and 22 ns)
. . . . . (about 0 cpu second for 1 parse)
```

	20	20.5	21.0	21.5	22
n1	5.0	4.5	4.0	3.5	3.0
n13	0.455	0.4124	0.3709	0.333	0.2993
n25	1.017	0.8513	0.6405	0.4589	0.3326

Interpreted as "What are the voltages at n1 and n13 and n25 between 20 and 22 ns?" A table is printed instead of a graph.

```
>> (what is the voltage at n1 5 ns after the voltage at n13
       equals 4 v)
. . . . . . . . . . . . . . . . (about 1 cpu second for  2 parses)
Node n1.  Time(s): (15)
   Voltage(s): (5.0)
```

Time-adverbial subordinate clauses can take numeric prefixes. Whereas the clause itself specifies a time-interval, the presence of the prefix results in a time-specification of a time-point.

```
>> (when is the voltage at n1 greater than 2 volts when the
       voltage at n13 equals 5 v)
. . . . . . . . . . . . . . . . . . . . . . (about 1 cpu second for 1
                                                   parse)

        |  6 |  8 |
---------------------
     n1 | 5.0 | 5.0 |
```

This sentence contains a headless relative clause. Only tense information can distinguish between the main and the subordinate clause. Such a sentence is also difficult to handle (especially for strictly case-frame parsers) because there are two fillers for the "temporal" case-role: the interrogative pronoun and the subordinate clause.

```
>> (at 15 ns which node is the voltage maximum at)
. . . . . . . . . . . (about 0 cpu second for 1 parse)
Node n1.  Time(s): (15)
   Voltage(s): (5.0)
```

This is a wh-fronted sentence. The noun-phrase "which-node" is actually the object of the trailing preposition "at". Although widely separated in the input, the two constituents have to be linked. Many natural language interfaces cannot handle this construction. Note also that the time-specification has been fronted.

```
>> (at what node is the voltage maximum after the voltage at n1
       reaches 3 v)
. . . . . . . . . . . . . . . . (about 1 cpu second for 1 parse)
Node n13.  Time(s): (8.0)
   Voltage(s): (5.166)
```

In this case, the fronted "wh" is a prepositional phrase.

```
>> (when does the voltage at n1 reach 5 v)
. . . . . . . . . . (about 0 cpu second for 1 parse)
Node n1.  Time(s): (6.0)
   Voltage(s): (5.0)
```

Cleoptra handles the auxiliary "do."

```
>> (at n13)
. . (about 0 cpu second for 1 parse)
Node n13.  Time(s): (0.0)
   Voltage(s): (5.0)
```

Interpreted as "When does the voltage at n13 reach 5 v?"

```
>> (does the voltage at n2 ever reach 3 v)
. . . . . . . . . . (about 0 cpu second for 1 parse)
No, never.
```

Again, tense information has to be utilized to recognize this sentence as a question.

```
>> (what is the voltage at n13 after 0.5 ns and before the
       voltage at n1 reaches 2 v)
. . . . . . . . . . . . . . . . . . . . . . . (about 3 cpu seconds for  2
                                                      parses)

          |   1.0 |   1.5 |   2.0 |   2.5 |   3.0 |
---------------------------------------------------
      n13 |   5.0 | 5.001 | 5.001 |   5.0 |   5.0 |
```

Conjoining two time-intervals results in a time-specification consisting of the intersection of the intervals.

```
>> (when is the voltage at n23 3 v)
. . . . . . . . . . (about 0 cpu second for 1 parse)
Node n23.  Time(s): (15)
   Voltage(s): (3)
```

This sentence is interpreted as "When is the voltage at n23 equal to 3 v?" This latter query would also be accepted by Cleopatra.

```
>> (what is the voltage at n13 after the voltage at n1 reaches
        2 v and before the voltage at n23 reaches 3 v)
. . . . . . . . . . . . . . . . . . . . . . .
(about 4 cpu seconds for  2 parses)

(volts)
5.38     |
5.047    |* * * * * * * * * * * *
4.714    |                        *
4.381    |                          *
4.048    |                            *
3.715    |                              *
3.382    |                                *
3.049    |                                  *
2.716    |                                    *
2.383    |                                      *
2.05     |                                        * *
1.717    |                                            * *
1.384    |                                                *
          +---+---+---+---+---+---+---+---+---+---+---+---+---+
         3.0 4.0 5.0 6.0 7.0 8.0 9.010.011.012.013.014.0  15  (ns)

LEGEND:  * : n13
```

Two subordinate clauses are conjoined.

```
>> (what is the voltage at n1 plus the voltage at n13)
. . . . . . . . . . . . (about 1 cpu second for  2 parses)
(volts)
11.16    |
10.16    |           *******
9.16     |         **       **
8.16     |       **           ***
7.16     |     **                *****
6.16     |   **                       ********
5.16     |****                                *****
4.16     |                                         **
3.16     |                                           **
2.16     |                                             **
1.16     |                                               **
0.16     |                                                 *
          +----+----+----+----+----+----+----+----+----+----+
         0.0  2.5  5.0  7.5 10.0 12.5 15.0 17.5 20.0 22.5 25.0  (ns)

 LEGEND:   * : **complex**
```

*Cleopatra allows the use of infix arithmetic functions. Note that the graph-marker is labelled as "**complex**", since it is not a single node that is being graphed.*

```
>> (what is the sum of the voltages at n1 and n13)
. . . . . . . . . . . . . (about 1 cpu second for 1 parse)
(volts)
11.16   |
10.16   |            *******
9.16    |          **       **
8.16    |        **           ***
7.16    |      **                *****
6.16    |    **                       ********
5.16    |****                                 *****
4.16    |                                          **
3.16    |                                            **
2.16    |                                              **
1.16    |                                                **
0.16    |                                                  *
         +----+----+----+----+----+----+----+----+----+----+
        0.0  2.5  5.0  7.5 10.0 12.5 15.0 17.5 20.0 22.5 25.0  (ns)

LEGEND:  * : **complex**
```

Prefix arithmetic functions can also be used.

```
>> (the difference)
. . (about 0 cpu second for 1 parse)
(volts)
5.0      |                                         *
4.0      |                              ********** **
3.0      |                         *****             **
2.0      |                      ***                    **
1.0      |                   ***                         **
0.0      |           ********                              **
-1.0     |         **
-2.0     |       **
-3.0     |     **
-4.0     |    **
-5.0     |****
          +----+----+----+----+----+----+----+----+----+----+
         0.0  2.5  5.0  7.5 10.0 12.5 15.0 17.5 20.0 22.5 25.0  (ns)

LEGEND:  * : **complex**
```

Interpreted as "What is the difference of the voltages at n1 and n13?" Ellipsis can be used for arithmetic functions too.

```
>> (when is voltage n1 greater voltage n2)
. . . . . . . . . (about 1 cpu second for  2 parses)
(volts)
5.328    |
4.995    |         *****************************
4.662    |        *                              *
4.329    |
3.996    |       *                                *
3.663    |      *                                  *
3.33     |
2.997    |     *                                    *
2.664    |    *                                      *
2.331    |
1.998    |   *                                        *
1.665    |  *                                          *
1.332    |
0.999    | *                                            *
0.666    |*                                              *
0.333    |
0.0      |                                                *
          +----+----+----+----+----+----+----+----+----+
        1.5  4.0  6.5  9.0 11.5 14.0 16.5 19.0 21.5 24.0   (ns)

LEGEND:  * : n1
```

This is an example of a "terse" expression. Articles and prepositions are missing, but the sentence is processed nevertheless.

```
>> (when voltage n1 reaches 3 v)
. . . . . . . (about 1 cpu second for  2 parses)
Node n1.  Time(s): (4.0)
   Voltage(s): (3.0)
```

Another example of a terse expression. Note that this query could more naturally be a subordinate clause of a complex sentence: "When voltage n1 reaches 3 v, what is voltage n2?" Cleopatra can handle such complex questions too, and it is because of its parallelism that it is not led astray here.

```
>> .abbrev > (greater than)
```

This defines an abbreviation. The symbol ">" stands for "greater than".

```
>> .abbrev vn (voltage at)
```

The symbol "vn" stands for "voltage at".

```
>> (when is vn n1 > vn n2)
. . . . . . . . . . . . . (about 1 cpu second for 1 parse)
(volts)
5.328   |
4.995   |         ******************************
4.662   |        *                              *
4.329   |
3.996   |       *                                *
3.663   |      *                                  *
3.33    |
2.997   |     *                                    *
2.664   |    *                                      *
2.331   |
1.998   |   *                                        *
1.665   |  *                                          *
1.332   |
0.999   | *                                            *
0.666   |*                                              *
0.333   |
0.0     |                                                *
         +----+----+----+----+----+----+----+----+----+
       1.5  4.0  6.5  9.0 11.5 14.0 16.5 19.0 21.5 24.0   (ns)

LEGEND:  * : n1
```

Interpreted as "When is voltage at n1 greater than voltage at n2?"

```
>> abbrev = (equal)
```

The symbol "=" stands for "equal".

```
>> (when vn n1 = vn n13)
. . . . . . . . . (about 1 cpu second for 1 parse)

         |      5 |      6 |      8 |     24 |
----------------------------------------------
      n1 |  4.995 |    5.0 |  4.999 | 0.1669 |
```

Interpreted as "When voltage at n1 equal voltage at n13?"

Appendix B
An Exercise in Extension

In numerous informal presentations of Cleopatra, one criticism has frequently surfaced: Since the parsing mechanism of Cleopatra, and the integration procedures in particular, are so complex, are not extensions of coverage extremely difficult to implement? This appendix provides a constructive proof to the contrary. We will describe how we extended Cleopatra to handle imperatives, such as *Display the voltage at n1.*

We are only interested in handling imperatives; therefore, the lexical entry for *display* need not indicate any tense information:

```
(((*display) (generic-verbs-1)))
```

The dictionary entry for **display* was derived by analogy with an existing dictionary entry for another verb, **reach*. Here is the dictionary entry for **reach*:

```
{
 [id: vXXXXX]
 [pos: v]
 [name: reach]
 [tns:]
 [mode:]
 [aux:]
 [voice:]
 [x-v:]
 [cases: (subj
           (lambda (x)
                   (is-feature x 'function-noun))
           before-v)
         (obj
           (lambda (x)
                   (is-feature x 'quantity))
           after-v)]
 [case-fills:]
 [pending:]
 [connections:]
 [attachments:]
 [status: open]
 [features: v-class1]
 [eval: !reach!]
}
```

Like *reach*, *display* also has two nuclear case-roles; however, we call the first one *agent* instead of *subj*, since there is a notion of agency involved with the subject of *display*. Since *display* can be the verb of an imperative sentence while *reach* (in the sense we are using it) cannot, we added a relevant feature to the dictionary entry for **display*. We did not need to change *v-class1* to something else. (If we had effected such a change, then the constraints associated with the noun-frame for *voltage* would have had to be slightly modified.) Here is the dictionary entry for **display*:

```
{
 [id: v00001]
 [pos: v]
 [name: display]
 [tns:]
 [mode:]
 [aux:]
 [voice:]
 [x-v:]
 [cases:
     (agent (lambda (x) (is-value x '*CLEO*))
            before-v)
     (obj (lambda (x) (is-feature x 'quantity))
          after-v)]
 [case-fills:]
 [pending:]
 [connections:]
 [attachments:]
 [status: open]
 [features: v-class1 imperative-ok]
 [eval: !display!]
}
```

We also composed a case-frame for Cleopatra itself, making it a global variable called **CLEO**:

```
{
 [id: I00001]
 [pos: case]
 [value: *CLEO*]
 [type:]
 [x-v:]
 [cases-for:
     (agent (lambda (x) (is-feature x 'v-class1))
            before-v)]
 [connections:]
 [attachments:]
 [features:]
 [lf: !*CLEO*]
}
```

Later on, such a case-frame could be used as a referent for *you*. In its present role **CLEO** is used as a dummy agent for imperatives.

One further modification was required before imperatives could be parsed. At the end of the integration procedure *generic-verbs-1*, there is a call to a procedure *pre-cases-done*. Previously this procedure merely added the feature *post-cases* to the new verb-frame and appended the verb-frame to **frames**. The following clause was added: If the verb-frame has the feature *imperative-ok*, and if the *before-v* case-role of the verb-frame has not been filled and does not have a possible filler on the *pending:* slot, then add **CLEO** as a filler for this case-role, and add *imperative* to the *mode:* slot.

Finally, the semantic interpretation procedure *!display!* was written:

1. If the verb-frame does not have *imperative* on its *mode:* slot, then indicate that a non-implemented construction (a non-imperative agentive sentence) has been encountered and terminate the procedure.

2. Get the *obj*, *temporal*, and *p-locative* case-fillers.

3. If the *p-locative* filler is present, then evaluate the filler and assert the returned value as locative information. Else assert the locative information, if any, from the parent (calling) frame.

4. If the *temporal* filler is present, then evaluate the filler and assert the returned value as temporal information. Else assert the temporal information, if any, from the parent frame.

5. Evaluate the *obj* filler with the asserted locative and temporal information, if any, and return the result.

A thorough understanding of Cleoptara is a prerequisite for implementing new constructions. However, once familiarity with Cleopatra is gained, incorporating new constructions is fairly straightforward. The above extension was implemented in less than two (man-)hours.

References

[1] Arens, Yigal.
Using language and context in the analysis of text.
In *Proceedings of the 7th International Joint Conference on Artificial Intelligence*, pages 52-57. 1981.

[2] Barbacci, M.R.
Instruction Set Processor Specification (ISPS): the notation and its applications.
IEEE Trans. Computers C-30(1):24-40, Jan., 1981.

[3] Barr, Avron and Edward A. Feigenbaum.
The Handbook of Artificial Intelligence.
William Kaufmann, Inc., Los Altos, California, 1981.

[4] Biermann, Alan W., Bruce W. Ballard, and Anne H. Sigmon.
An experimental study of natural language programming.
International Journal of Man-Machine Studies 18:71-87, 1983.

[5] Bierwisch, Manfred.
On Classifying Semantic Features.
In Bierwisch and Heidolph (editors), *Progress in Linguistics.* Mouton, The Hague, 1970.

[6] Bobrow, Robert J., and Bonnie L. Webber.
Knowledge representation for syntactic/semantic processing.
In *Proceedings of the 1st AAAI Conference*, pages 316-323. 1980.

[7] Brown, John Seely and Richard R. Burton.
Multiple Representations of Knowledge for Tutorial Reasoning.
In Daniel G. Bobrow and Allan Collins (editors), *Representation and Understanding*, pages 311-349. Academic Press, 1975.

[8] Bushnell, Michael L.
Delilah II -- An Enhanced Menu-Driven Input Processor.
Research Report CMUCAD-83-7, SRC-CMU Center for Computer-Aided Design, Department of Electrical and Computer Engineering, Carnegie-Mellon University, February, 1983.

[9] Bushnell, Michael L.
The Organization of an Effective Silicon-Chip Design System.
Ph.D. Proposal to the Department of Electrical and Computer Engineering, Carnegie-Mellon University. August, 1984.

[10] Carbonell, Jaime G. et al.
XCALIBUR Project Report 1
Computer Science Department, Carnegie-Mellon University, 1983.

[11] Carbonell, Jaime G., and Philip J. Hayes.
Recovery strategies for parsing extragrammatical language.
American Journal of Computational Linguistics 9(3-4):123-146, July-December, 1983.

[12] Charniak, Eugene.
The case-slot identity theory.
Cognitive Science 5:285-292, 1981.

[13] Chomsky, Noam.
Syntactic Structures.
Mouton, The Hague, 1957.

[14] Chomsky, Noam.
Aspects of the Theory of Syntax.
The M.I.T. Press, 1965.
Page references are to the paperback edition.

[15] Chomsky, Noam.
Reflections on Language.
Pantheon Books, 1975.
Page references are to the paperback edition.

[16] Chomsky, Noam.
Lectures on Government and Binding.
Foris, Dordrecht, 1981.

[17] Small, Steven, Gary Cottrell, and Lokenda Shastri.
Toward connectionist parsing.
In *Proceedings of the American Association for Artificial Intelligence*, pages 247-250. 1982.

[18] Culicover, Peter W.
Syntax.
Academic Press, 1976.

[19] Dasarathy, B., David S. Prerau, and James H. Vellenga.
The system compiler.
In *Proceedings of the 1983 IEEE International Symposium on Circuits and Systems*, pages 530-533. IEEE, 1983.

[20] Davis, Randall.
Interactive transfer of expertise: acquisition of new inference rules.
Artificial Intelligence 12(2):121-157, 1979.
Reprinted in [75].

[21] Director, S.W., et al.
A design methodology and computer aids for digital VLSI systems.
IEEE Transactions on Circuits and Systems CAS-28(7):634-645, July, 1981.

[22] Dreyfus, Hubert L.
What Computers Can't Do.
Harper and Row, 1979.
Page references are to the paperback edition.

[23] Duda, R., J. Gaschnig, and P. Hart.
Model Design in the Prospector Consultant System for Mineral Exploration.
In Michie, D. (editor), *Expert Systems in the Microelectronic Age*, pages 153-167. Edinburgh University Press, 1979.
Reprinted in [75].

[24] Erman, Lee, Frederick Hayes-Roth, Victor Lesser, and D. Raj Reddy.
The Hearsay-II speech understanding system: integrating knowledge to resolve uncertainty.
Computing Surveys 12(2):213-253, 1980.
Reprinted in [75].

[25] Fain, Jill, Jaime G. Carbonell, Philip J. Hayes, and Steven N. Minton.
MULTIPAR: a robust entity-oriented parser.
In *Proceedings of the 7th Annual Conference of the Cognitive Science Society.* August, 1985.

[26] Fillmore, Charles J.
The case for case.
Universals in Linguistic Theory.
Holt, Rinehart and Winston, 1968.

[27] Fillmore, Charles J.
The case for case reopened.
Syntax and Semantics: Volume 8--Grammatical Relations.
Academic Press, 1977.

[28] Fitter, M.
Toward more "natural" interactive systems.
International Journal of Man-Machine Studies 11:339-350, 1979.

[29] Foderaro, John.
The FRANZ Lisp Manual
The University of California, Berkeley, 1979.

[30] Fodor, Jerry A., and Jerrold J. Katz.
The structure of a semantic theory.
Language 39:170-210, 1963.

[31] Gazdar, Gerald, Ewan Klein, Geoffrey Pullum, and Ivan Sag.
Generalized Phrase Structure Grammar.
Harvard University Press, 1985.

[32] Gibbs, Raymond W., Jr.
literal meaning and psychological theory.
Cognitive Science 8:275-304, 1984.

[33] Green, Bert F., Alice K. Wolf, Carol Chomsky, and Kenneth Laughery.
Baseball: An Automatic Question Answerer.
In Feigenbaum, Edward A., and Julian Feldman (editors), *Computers and Thought*, pages 207-216. McGraw-Hill, 1963.

[34] Greenberg, Joseph H.
Essays in Linguistics.
University of Chicago Press, 1957.

[35] Grosz, Barbara J.
Discourse Knowledge.
In Donald E. Walker (editor), *Understanding Spoken Language*, chapter 4, pages 229-340. Elsevier North-Holland, Inc., 1978.

[36] Hayes, Philip J., and Jaime G. Carbonell.
Multi-strategy construction-specific parsing for flexible data base query and update.
In *Proceedings of the 7th International Joint Conference on Artificial Intelligence*, pages 432-439. 1981.

[37] Hayes, Philip J. and George V. Mouradian.
Flexible parsing.
American Journal of Computational Linguistics 7(4):232-242, October-December, 1981.

[38] Hendrix, Gary G., Earl D. Sacerdoti, Daniel Sagalowicz, and Jonathan Slocum.
Developing a natural language interface to complex data.
ACM Transactions on Database Systems 3(2):105-147, June, 1978.

[39] Hill, I.D.
Wouldn't it be nice if we could write computer programs in ordinary English--or would it?
The Computer Bulletin 16(6):306-312, June, 1972.

[40] Hirst, Graeme.
Discourse-oriented anaphora resolution in natural language understanding: a review.
American Journal of Computational Linguistics 7(2):85-98, April-June, 1981.

[41] Hsu, Kathy.
Delilah 3 -- An Improved User-Interface.
Master's thesis, Department of Electrical and Computer Engineering, Carnegie-Mellon University, 1984.

[42] Kaplan, R., and J. Bresnan.
Lexical-Functional Grammar: A Formal System for Grammatical Representation.
In J. Bresnan (editor), *The Mental Representation of Grammatical Relations*. The M.I.T. Press, 1982.

[43] Katz, Jerrold J., and Paul M. Postal.
An Integrated Theory of Linguistic Descriptions.
MIT Press, 1964.

[44] Katz, Jerrold J.
Philosophy of Language.
Harper and Row, 1966.

[45] Kiparsky, Paul and Carol Kiparsky.
Fact.
In Bierwisch and Heidolph (editors), *Progress in Linguistics*. Mouton, The Hague, 1970.

[46] Kwasny, Stan C., and Norman K. Sondheimer.
Relaxation techniques for parsing grammatically ill-formed input in natural language understanding systems.
American Journal of Computational Linguistics 7(2):99-108, April-June, 1981.

[47] Ledgard, Henry, John A. Whiteside, Andrew Singer, and William Seymour.
The natural language of interactive studies.
Communications of the ACM 23(10), October, 1980.

[48] Lehmann, H.
interpretation of natural language in an information system.
IBM Journal of Research and Development 22(5):560-572, September, 1978.

[49] Lesmo, Leonardo, Daniela Magnani, and Piero Torasso.
A deterministic analyser for the interpretation of natural language commands.
In *Proceedings of the 7th International Joint Conference on Artificial Intelligence*, pages 440-442. 1981.

[50] Lyons, John.
Introduction to Theoretical Linguistics.
Cambridge University Press, 1968.

[51] Marcus, Mitchell P.
A Theory of Syntactic Recognition for Natural Language.
MIT Press, 1980.

[52] Milne, Robert William.
Predicting garden path sentences.
Cognitive Science 6(4), October-December, 1982.

[53] Minsky, Marvin.
A Framework for Representing Knowledge.
In Patrick H. Winston (editor), *The Psychology of Computer Vision*. McGraw-Hill, 1975.

[54] Nagel, L.W.
SPICE 2: A Computer Program to Simulate Semiconductor Circuits.
Technical Report Memo No. ERL-M520, Electr. Research Laboratory, U.C. Berkeley, May, 1975.

[55] Nash, J.D.
21st DAC - workshop / panel reviews.
ACM SIGDA Newsletter 14(3):9, 1984.

[56] Nash-Webber, Bonnie Lynn and Raymond Reiter.
Anaphora and logical-form: on formal meaning representations for natural language.
In *Proceedings of the Fifth International Joint Conference on Artificial Intelligence*, pages 121-131. August, 1977.

[57] Perlman, G.
Natural artificial languages.
International Journal of Man-Machine Studies 20(4), April, 1984.

[58] Peters, P. Stanley, Jr., and R.W. Ritchie.
On restricting the base component of transformational grammars.
Information and Control 18(5):483-501, 1971.

[59] Peters, P. Stanley, Jr., and R.W. Ritchie.
On the generative power of transformational grammars.
Information Sciences 6(1):49-83, 1973.

[60] Plath, W.J.
REQUEST: a natural language question-answering system.
IBM Journal of Research and Development 20:326-335, July, 1976.

[61] Pollio, Howard R., Michael S. Fabrizi, Abigail Sills, and Michael K. Smith.
Need metaphoric comprehension take longer than literal comprehension?
Journal of Psycholinguistic Research 13(3), 1984.

[62] Pylyshyn, Zenon W.
The role of competence theories in cognitive psychology.
Journal of Psycholinguistic Research 2(1):21-50, 1973.

[63] Schank, Roger C.
Conceptual Information Processing.
North-Holland, 1975.

[64] Searle, John R.
Indirect speech acts.
Syntax and Semantics: Volume 3--Speech Acts.
Academic Press, 1975.

[65] Shneiderman, B.
Software Psychology: Human Factors in Computer and Information Studies.
Winthrop, New York, 1980.

[66] Shortliffe, Edward H.
Consultation systems for physicians: the role of artificial intelligence techniques.
In *Proceedings of the Canadian Society for Computational Studies of Intelligence.* 1980.
Reprinted in [75].

[67] Sibuya, M., T. Fujisaki, and Y. Takao.
Noun-phrase model and natural query language.
IBM Journal of Research and Development 22(5):533-540, Spetember, 1978.

[68] Sidner, Candace L.
focusing for interpretation of pronouns.
American Journal of Computational Linguistics 7(4):217-231, October-December, 1981.

[69] Simon, Herbert A.
The Sciences of the Artificial.
The M.I.T. Press, 1969.

[70] Soames, Scott, and David M. Perlmutter.
Syntactic Argumentation and the Structure of English.
University of California Press, 1979.

[71] Spence, R.
Human factors in interactive graphics.
Computer Aided Design 8(1):49-53, 1976.

[72] Stageberg, Norman C.
Some Structural Ambiguities.
In Harold B. Allen (editor), *Readings in Applied English Linguistics.* Appleton-Century-Croft, 1964.

[73] Waltz, David L.
An English language question answering system for a large relational database.
Communications of the ACM 21(7):526-539, July, 1978.

[74] Waltz, David L., and Jordan B. Pollack.
Massively parallel parsing: a strongly interactive model of natural language interpretation.
Cognitive Science 9:51-74, 1985.

[75] Webber, Bonnie Lynn, and Nils J. Nilsson (editors).
Readings in Artificial Intelligence.
Tioga, Palo Alto, 1981.

[76] Weischedel, Ralph M., and Norman K. Sondheimer.
Meta-rules as a basis for processing ill-formed input.
American Journal of Computational Linguistics 9(3-4):161-177, July-December, 1983.

[77] Winograd, Terry.
Language as a Cognitive Process -- Volume I: Syntax.
Addison-Wesley, 1983.

[78] Wittgenstein, Ludwig.
Philosophical Investigations.
Macmillan, New York, 1958.

[79] Wong, Douglas.
Language comprehension in a problem solver.
In *Proceedings of the 7th International Joint Conference on Artificial Intelligence*, pages 7-12. 1981.

[80] Woods, W.A.
Transition network grammars for natural language analysis.
Communications of the ACM 3:591-606, 1970.

[81] Woods, W.A., R.M. Kaplan, and B. Nash-Webber.
The lunar sciences natural language information system: Final report.
Technical Report BBN Report No. 2378, Bolt, Beranek, and Newman, Inc., Cambridge, MA, 1972.

Index